LIVING AND LOVING TOGETHER

LIVING AND LOVING TOGETHER

A practical manual for better relationships

Dr Bob Montgomery, BA, PhD, MAPsS
and
Lynette Evans, BBSc, MPsych.

VIKING O'NEIL

Viking O'Neil
Penguin Books Australia Ltd
487 Maroondah Highway, PO Box 257
Ringwood, Victoria 3134, Australia
Penguin Books Ltd
Harmondsworth, Middlesex, England
Viking Penguin, A Division of Penguin Books USA Inc.
375 Hudson Street, New York, New York 10014, USA
Penguin Books Canada Limited
10 Alcorn Avenue, Toronto, Ontario, Canada M4V 1E4
Penguin Books (N.Z.) Ltd
182–190 Wairau Road, Auckland 10, New Zealand

First published by Nelson Publishers 1983
This edition by Penguin Books Australia 1989

5 7 9 10 8 6 4

Produced by Viking O'Neil
56 Claremont Street, South Yarra, Victoria 3141, Australia
A Division of Penguin Books Australia Ltd

Cover designed by David Constable
Typeset in 11 point California and 10 point Univers by Colset Pty Ltd
Printed in Australia by Australian Print Group, Maryborough

National Library of Australia
Cataloguing-in-Publication data

Montgomery, Bob, 1943–
Living and loving together.

Includes bibliographies.
ISBN 0 670 90154 7.

1. Marriage. 2. Interpersonal relations.
1. Evans, Lynette. II. Title.

306.8'7

Contents

To Professor Bob Weiss

*Head of the Marital Studies Unit,
Psychology Clinic, University of Oregon*

a good friend and pioneer

Introduction

What is this manual about?

This manual has two purposes:

1 It is intended to help couples in distressed relationships to work systematically on fixing up those relationships. This is called marital or relationship therapy.

2 It is intended to help couples who don't necessarily think their relationships have serious problems, but who think their relationships could be better, to work systematically on improving their relationships. This is called marriage or relationship enhancement.

If you are thinking of buying this manual, you should note now that to use it effectively will require you to make a systematic and sustained effort. We don't believe good relationships occur 'naturally', and we doubt that anyone will gain anything other than knowledge from simply reading this manual.

Knowledge is great stuff, and a necessary beginning for many successful enterprises, but it is the use that knowledge is put to that makes them successful. This is not a pop psychology book about love and marriage: it is a practical manual for people who are ready to do something to make their relationships better.

Many couples that come to us feel awkward or embarrassed about doing some of the structured exercises. Some are dismayed by how much work is required to make, and then keep, a good relationship.

These reactions reflect the lack of human relations education in our community. Research has shown how many of us bring quite unrealistic expectations to our relationships, shaped by such influences as movies, television and romantic novels. It is genuinely sad to see how many people believe that relationship success should come 'naturally' if you're 'in love'. Real world relationships are quite different, as our rising divorce rates show. People are not at all disenchanted with the idea of 'relatedness'. Surprisingly, more people are married now, in law or in fact, than ever before. But increasing numbers are disenchanted with their present relationships, and many marriages are second or third attempts at happiness.

Although more people than ever seek personal fulfilment and happiness through living together, there is no evidence that they are doing it with any more success. This sad situation undoubtedly results because they lack both factual information about relationships, and the chance to learn basic relationship skills.

This manual sets out to provide both:

factual information about relationships, to help you set realistic expectations of each other and of your relationship;

and concrete descriptions and examples of basic relationship skills, with many opportunities for you to practise them.

For those who wish to know more about the theory and research behind our approach to relationship therapy, we have included a short description at the back of this book, together with a guide for therapists.

IS THIS MANUAL FOR YOU?

As a self-help guide, this manual will be of most help to couples in which both partners want to work on the relationship, and there isn't all that much else wrong in their lives.

Self-help can be difficult to apply successfully, despite the grandiose claims you will see on the glossy pop psychology books currently flooding the market. Successful self-help requires close adherence to the advice in the self-help programme. What looks to you like a small change could, in fact, make a big difference to how the programme works.

If you try self-help and it doesn't work, see a properly trained counsellor. At the risk of making ourselves unpopular, let us state our belief that lay counsellors with brief training in marriage guidance offer valuable but limited assistance. They can provide, for comparatively little cost, a sympathetic ear and some useful advice, which is enough for some couples. But if you try marriage guidance counselling and it doesn't help, don't despair. We believe marital therapy is amongst the most complicated, and it requires a fully trained professional to deliver it.

Sometimes relationship problems are associated with individual problems in one or both of the partners. For example, one may be depressed, and this individual problem will interact with the problems in the relationship. The more depressed she feels, the more strain that puts on the marriage. The more strained the marriage, the more depressed she feels.

Or he may have a serious drinking problem, as a result of poor stress-coping skills. The more he drinks, the worse the marriage becomes. The more tense the home atmosphere, the more likely he is to escape to the pub.

It is doubtful whether either self-help or simple marriage guidance counselling will be effective in such complicated cases. In our experience, it is essential to tackle all of the problems, often simultaneously, to be successful in any.

Such broad therapy programmes can only be provided by a properly trained professional. We recommend a qualified clinical psychologist. This will usually be a person with a university post-graduate qualification in clinical psychology, or membership of the Clinical Board of the Australian Psychological Society. Beware of imitations!

If your counsellor or psychologist isn't noticeably helpful within a few visits, we encourage you to shop around. Not all helpers in the market are equally effective, and you have a right to effective assistance, whether you are paying for it directly by fee or indirectly by taxes.

We don't believe that effective therapy needs to take two years of reviewing your early childhood. In a typical marital therapy case, we expect to see the couple about six to eight times. We don't claim to work miracles; we do set them lots of assignments. So for one hour in therapy with us, they will spend many hours trying out their new relationship skills at home.

That's where this manual should be helpful even to those couples who do go to counselling or therapy. It sets out exactly the assignments we use to help couples master new relationship skills. Your counsellor or therapist may well find it useful for setting your homework. Discuss it with him.

Just as this manual alone is unlikely to help much in complicated cases of relationship problems, it also will offer limited help to the couple in which only one partner wants to use it. Relationships occur between people, not inside one or the other of the partners.

You can think of a relationship as a system, such as a car, and tinkering with one part of that system will of course influence the rest of the system to some extent. But there are very real limits to how much positive change one partner can bring into a relationship, while the other does nothing, or even obstructs the efforts of the first.

The very fact that one partner refuses to acknowledge the problems in the relationship, or refuses to work on them, tells you something about the state of that relationship, and its future chances.

This doesn't mean that you have to share 100 per cent commitment to, or faith in, the possibility of making the relationship better. In fact, when distressed couples come to therapy, they nearly always have mixed feelings.

'Gee, that used to be so good, and this was something we always shared. But, oh, that was dreadful, and how could he have done this to me. Will it ever work or won't it?'

We suggest that relationship therapy can be viewed in two ways. First, it gives you a good, practical chance of making the relationship work really well for both of you. It's a systematic approach to developing and keeping a relationship you're both glad to be in.

Secondly, it is also a decision-making process. If you both give a good honest try to the exercises in this manual, and your relationship doesn't improve, that's telling you something. Maybe it's time you either saw a properly trained counsellor or therapist, or accepted that you're in the wrong relationship, and did something constructive about that.

Unfortunately, present indications are that separation and divorce often are hurtful for the people involved, adults and children. The end of a relationship will probably always be hurtful, but it doesn't have to be destructive.

About two thirds of the couples we see in relationship therapy eventually stay together, and tell us that their relationships have improved considerably. Even more promising, they often also tell us that they can see how much better their relationships can be, and how to achieve this.

About one third decide to end their relationships. This usually seems to be a realistic decision, more so than dragging out the misery of an unworkable relationship. We have noticed that the more marital therapy these couples have done, the more constructively they handle the ends of their relationships.

So, the best advice to those in doubt and dilemma over the future of their relationships is to try to make them work. If that effort is successful, you have a better relationship. If it isn't successful, you have a decision which you can make with a clearer conscience.

BEFORE YOU BEGIN

Self-esteem

Low self-esteem is an individual problem that causes a lot of dissatisfaction in intimate relationships. We will mention a number of times throughout this book that self-esteem, or feeling good about yourself, is an important prerequisite for enjoying and behaving successfully in a long-term relationship.

By self-esteem, we mean how you see yourself. If you generally see yourself as a lovable person who does well in some areas of life, is able to cope with most problems, and generally feels pleased and happy about yourself, then you would have good self-esteem. Poor self-esteem is usually the result of thinking of yourself as a failure, only noticing the things that you do badly and actually having bad things happen to you. So even a person who generally has positive

Inside Woody Allen

thoughts about himself will suffer from lowered self-esteem in a situation where a large number of negative events are occurring.

For instance, if you have a good self-esteem but become involved in a very poor relationship, your self-esteem will suffer. If, on the other hand, you have negative thoughts about yourself, for example, 'No-one could ever love me', then no matter how good the relationship, or how hard your partner tries to prove she loves you, you will not believe that you are lovable. The old saying 'you have to love yourself before you can love anyone else' is true in the sense that if you do not see yourself as lovable then you are going to find it very hard to believe that anyone else could love you. This disbelief in your own lovability will always be an obstacle to your success in intimate relationships.

If you have doubts about your attractiveness in the context of your current relationship, then working through this book, paying particular attention to dealing with bad feelings (see Chapter 5), should be enough to help you change your poor self-esteem in the context of the relationship.

If your poor self-esteem is the result of a very bad relationship, then changing the relationship for the better, or making the decision to leave the relationship, should be enough for you to regain your self-esteem.

If, however, your poor self-esteem is more general, not just associated with feeling unsure about yourself in the context of this relationship but an overall uncertainty about yourself in all areas of your life, including your relationship, then this book alone, will not be sufficient. We doubt that people with overall, poor self-esteem can be helped by a self-help book. We would normally recommend that, if you feel you are in this position, you seek professional counselling, from a properly qualified clinical psychologist (see above).

If you do want to try self-help, then the book, *Like Yourself and Others Will Too* by A. Twerski (published by Prentice-Hall), may be a place to start. If the book isn't helpful we encourage you to seek professional help because lack of self-esteem is a problem that you can do something about.

Secondary relationships

In addition to both of you wanting to work on the relationship, we think you both need to be able to concentrate on that task without undue distraction. So we suggest to couples in therapy that they agree to a moratorium on secondary intimate relationships, while they work on their primary relationship with each other.

It is not unusual for one of the partners in a distressed relationship to be involved in a secondary relationship. Often it is the discovery of this secondary relationship that appears to have precipitated distress in the primary relationship. Frankly, we doubt this interpretation.

We have often seen people become involved in secondary relationships because there is something lacking or wrong in their primary relationships. We have not seen primary relationships suddenly develop deficiencies or serious problems because one of the partners had begun a secondary relationship.

This is not intended as a simple-minded endorsement of

secondary relationships. Your expectations of each other so far as secondary relationships are concerned are something for you to decide. It is intended to discourage you from overreacting destructively to the discovery of an 'affair'.

If an 'affair' has suddenly caused you to take stock of what's wrong in your relationship, and that gives you the chance of putting it right, then in a very real sense you owe it a debt of thanks.

None the less, if you have both decided to work on your primary relationship with each other, then we strongly suggest you call at least a temporary halt to any secondary relationships. Otherwise you run a strong risk of the comparison game.

This involves you endlessly comparing your two partners, primary and secondary, on all sorts of characteristics, to try to decide which one you 'really' love or would be 'happier' with. The trouble with these sorts of comparisons is that they are totally unfair and invalid.

Usually you will be meeting your secondary partner for only brief periods, for fun activities, like dates or sex. No housework, no kids, no mortgages, none of the problems that occur in all long-term relationships.

It's like comparing a punnet of fresh strawberries with a sack of potatoes. They're both for eating, but one is for immediate consumption to be enjoyed briefly, before it goes off. The other is more a reliable investment for your future nutritional needs, perhaps less exciting, but probably welcome one cold winter's night. They're too different to compare meaningfully.

In Chapter 9 we'll discuss ending relationships. For now, let us foreshadow our advice there by discouraging you from leaving one primary relationship in order to go straight into another. You are doing your new relationship no favours to start it that way.

For now, you must agree to put your relationship efforts exclusively into your primary relationship. Later, when your primary relationship is working better, you may need to negotiate agreement over the nature and extent of any secondary relationships. If it doesn't get better, at least you will know you gave it an honest try.

Sex and sexism

Many of the problems in relationships are triggered by the uncritical acceptance of popular beliefs and attitudes which are ultimately anti-relationship. We will encourage you to look at these, and their influence on your relationship, in Chapter 1. These popular myths set people up for relationship distress and disappointment.

Now we want to single out the collection of myths and attitudes summarised in the concept of the double standard: the belief that men and women are immutably different in a number of ways that necessitate their filling markedly different and rigid roles in society.

Although the double standard has often been presented as systematically favouring men to the disadvantage of women, we believe that both sexes lose under it; they just lose different things. Much relationship distress, which hurts both partners, stems from double standard assumptions.

We are therefore unwilling consciously to support such assumptions by adopting sexist language practices, however traditional these may be. Women and men take part in relationships, and what we have to say will usually apply equally to both.

On the other hand, it is cumbersome and paper-consuming always to talk about 'he or she' and 'hers or his'. Using 'them' or 'theirs' when you really mean one person is just bad English.

Our solution, as you may have already noticed, has been to alternate the sex of our personal pronouns, except when doing so would be inappropriate. So most of the time, for 'he' you can also read 'she', for 'hers' you can also read 'his', and so on, unless the change makes it silly. We think you will notice those occasions.

If you find this unsettling, we think that's probably good. It is probably showing you how unconsciously you have accepted traditional discriminatory practices, which may well be contributing to any distress in your relationship. Besides, we found we got used to it after a while. So can you.

Equally, we think that what we have to say probably applies to 'him and him' and 'her and her'. Although the determinants of success for homosexual relationships have been much less studied than those for heterosexual relationships, our clinical experience has been that the same problems occur, and the same solutions work, in both kinds of relationships.

WHAT THIS MANUAL COVERS

After this introduction, we will consider in detail the following topics.

1 Myths and facts about relationships
2 Making relationships more rewarding
3 Communicating better
4 Improving your sexual relationship
5 Cutting out fights
6 Solving problems together
7 Negotiating behaviour changes
8 Coping with kids
9 What to do if it all doesn't work

All couples should begin by reading Chapter 1, and completing the discussion exercises in that chapter. The aim of this is to help you begin the process of improving your relationship with realistic expectations.

After Chapter 1, the best order in which you do the remaining chapters depends on which areas of your relationship most need improvement. If you are going to a marital counsellor or therapist, then you should be guided by her advice.

If you are using the manual to guide self-help, you will first need to do some self-analysis, to identify the areas in your relationship that most need improvement.

ASSESSING THE STRENGTHS AND WEAKNESSES IN YOUR RELATIONSHIP

You may feel that you know these pretty well already. After all, isn't that why you've decided to do some self-help improvement of the relationship?

Ultimately you will be the best (and only) judge of what you want and will accept from your relationship, and we would never want to take that role from you. But we have found that many people wrongly identify the problems in their relationships.

This is partly due to the lack of human relations education in the community, so many people are unaware of what really goes on in a successful relationship. We will attack the lack of realistic expectations directly in Chapter 1, but in the meantime you will have to be willing to accept a little guidance in assessing your relationship.

Couples coming to therapy often have long lists of complaints about each other and the relationship. Although these complaints are sincere expressions of feelings, they are usually too vague or generalised to lead to productive change.

On the other hand, some couples assure us that they have 'perfect communication' when what actually happens is that they talk to each other a lot, which is good, but never about contentious issues in the relationship, which is bad.

Similarly, some couples will quite correctly report that they 'never fight', but this peace is achieved by further avoiding of issues, not by a lack of them.

The situation is confused further by people's understandable comparisons of their relationships with those of friends or family. 'Well, compared to our friends, our relationship is pretty good.' This may be quite true, but it rests on a questionable assumption. This is that your friends' relationships are as good as relationships can be, and they are therefore a good standard against which to measure yours. Our rising divorce rates cast serious doubt on this assumption.

In any case, the question really is whether or not your relationship is, or can be, good enough for **you** to want to stay in it, not your friends. So both of you try the following assessment, to see how well you can fit this standard self-help programme to your individual needs.

If you have trouble answering these questions, completing the two questionnaires at the end of this chapter may help you to be more specific. If you want this help, do the questionnaires now, and then come back to this point.

Not enough common interests and shared pleasure?

How many enjoyable activities or recreations do you do together?

How often do you have a date, just as a couple (that is, no family, no friends, just the two of you)?

How rewarding is your sexual relationship now?

If your answers to these questions are mostly negative, you should emphasise Chapters 2 and 4. If you do not identify any other major problem areas, you could usefully work through the manual in simple numerical order, from 1 to 8.

Communication problems?

How much does each of you think that the other understands your point of view and feelings on important issues?

Are you easily and comfortably able to share good feelings and give each other compliments?

Are you easily and comfortably able to share bad feelings and give each other constructive criticism?

If your answers to these questions are mostly negative, you should emphasise Chapter 3, and it may be helpful if you did Chapter 3 before going on with Chapter 2 and the rest of the book.

Too many fights?

Are you having frequent arguments?

When tension occurs in the relationship, does one of you withdraw from the discussion and stay sullenly quiet for a while?

When an argument starts, do you find yourself thinking, 'Here we go again'?

Have your arguments included physical violence?

If your answers to these questions indicate that fighting, or the risk of it, is a problem in your relationship, you should emphasise Chapters 3 and 5. After Chapter 1, do both of these before you go on with the rest of the manual.

Self-help seems to be hardest for couples with fighting problems. Often they get caught in what we call a 'stand-off': 'You do something to prove your good intentions, before I will do anything.' While both think like this, nothing (good) happens.

Do **not** use this manual or its suggestions as fresh ammunition. If it becomes just another weapon to hit each other over the head with – 'You didn't do what the book says!' 'Yes, I did. It's you who's not following the instructions!' – then you will lose any possible benefit from the programme.

If you can't break your stand-offs, following Chapters 3 and 5, and use the manual co-operatively to solve your problems, see a qualified counsellor or therapist.

Is there a power struggle?

Do you think that your partner shows consideration for your feelings, wishes and opinions?
Are major decisions the result of discussions between you?
Are there recurring issues that you keep fighting over, without ever resolving them?

If you answer 'No', 'No', 'Yes' to these questions, you should emphasise Chapters 6 and 7, but you will get the most out of these if you have done Chapters 2 to 5 beforehand. This means exercising some patience and postponing working on these problems, until you have the prerequisite communication skills and you are improving the positive side of your relationship.

This advice of exercising patience really applies to all users of the manual. As you can now see, there are a number of skills in making a good relationship, and you cannot master them all at once. Some, like communication, are really prerequisites for others, like problem-solving.

Similarly, as you enhance the pleasure in the relationship, it is easier to see problems in a more sensible perspective, to decide which ones are really worth raising, and to feel more motivated to solve them.

So, if working on the earlier chapters raises issues that cannot be solved without the skills covered in later chapters, try to be patient. Put those problems into the waiting-to-be-solved basket. They will make good starting points for later exercises.

Your answers to the following questions will also be used in the practical exercises in different chapters, so take the time to write out your answers now.

1 What would you like to see changed in your relationship? (Try to be specific.)

2 What are the strengths in your relationship? (What would you like to see retained or strengthened?)

3 What would you like to change about yourself, for the sake of the relationship? (Again, try to be specific.)

4 What would you like to change about your partner, for the sake of the relationship? (Specific again, please.)

You may feel that some of the chapters are irrelevant or unnecessary for you. For example, you may have no children, and so Chapter 8 won't be of much practical help to you (at least until you do have children, if you do).

But be wary of skipping much. An area of your relationship that is not problematic may still be able to be strengthened. It's much easier to prevent problems by acquiring or strengthening the relevant skills, than it is to solve them later when you are distressed and discouraged.

After all, you are working on a relationship in which you presumably intend to spend a fair bit of time. It's worth putting in a few hours now, even on chapters that don't appear so necessary for you, to protect that future.

Finally, if you try the programme and your relationship isn't getting better, or at least good enough to make it really worth your while staying in it, then you should work through Chapter 9.

TWO QUESTIONNAIRES TO HELP YOU TO DECIDE WHICH ARE THE MOST PRESSING PROBLEMS IN YOUR RELATIONSHIP

It is important that you answer the questions below as accurately as possible. This is not a test to determine how good your relationship is. It is an assessment of where your relationship stands at the moment. The rest of the book will then help you to improve upon your relationship in an order that should be most beneficial to you as individuals.

Questionnaire 1

This schedule is designed to give you information about how comfortable you feel about various behaviours that sometimes occur in intimate relationships. If feelings of discomfort are preventing you from doing things that you would like to do, and which would contribute to the success of your relationship, those feelings would be appropriate targets to change. Please read the descriptions of the behaviours below, and rate how comfortable you feel (or think you would feel) behaving that way with your partner now. Use a 7-point scale, in which 1 = very uncomfortable and 7 = completely comfortable.

1 Affectionately saying to your partner, 'I love you'. ( )
2 Your partner affectionately saying to you, 'I love you'. ( )
3 Telling your partner that you feel very bad about something s/he did. ( )
4 Telling your partner that you really appreciate something s/he did. ( )
5 Giving your partner a surprise gift. ( )
6 Receiving a surprise gift from your partner. ( )
7 Your partner telling you that s/he feels very bad about something you did. ( )
8 Your partner telling you that s/he really appreciates something you did. ( )
9 You touching your partner affectionately. ( )
10 Your partner touching you affectionately. ( )
11 Kissing each other. ( )
12 Seeing your partner undressed. ( )
13 Your partner seeing you undressed. ( )
14 Making love together. ( )
15 Listening to your partner when you are upset with something s/he did. ( )

16 Listening to your partner when s/he is upset with something you did. ( )

17 Stopping the conversation when you are upset. ( )

18 Stopping the conversation when your partner is upset. ( )

19 When you and your partner have very different points of view on an important topic. ( )

20 Discussing a topic again that you and your partner have previously disagreed over. ( )

21 Bringing up a topic which you and your partner have previously disagreed over. ( )

22 Resolving important differences in your relationship with your partner. ( )

23 Accepting a solution suggested by your partner, to resolve a problem in your relationship. ( )

Now please indicate how strongly you believe the following statements. Again, use a 7-point scale, where 1 = 'don't believe it at all' and 7 = 'completely believe it'.

24 My partner sees me as physically and sexually attractive. ( )

25 My partner sees me as an interesting person. ( )

26 I see my partner as physically and sexually attractive. ( )

27 I see my partner as an interesting person. ( )

28 My feelings and opinions are considered by my partner. ( )

29 We both participate equally in resolving problems. ( )

30 When we have a difference to resolve we take time to find a solution that suits both of us. ( )

Questionnaire 2

Now go on to these questions.

For this section we would like you to think back to the last time the situations described below occurred in your relationship. Then we would like you to choose the most appropriate answer. The answers may not always closely match what actually happened, but choose the answer nearest to what happened.

1 Last time you and your partner shared an activity together or went out together:

(a) You both really enjoyed yourselves.

(b) You were unsure whether your partner enjoyed him/herself but you were happy to be together.

(c) You enjoyed the activity but at times got on each other's nerves.

(d) It was a real flop.

2 Last time you and your partner discussed an important issue in your relationship:

    (a) You were both able to accept each other's point of view even if it was different. The discussion went well.

    (b) You felt that your partner really understood what you were saying but seemed to be intent on putting across his/her point of view.

    (c) You felt that your partner's point of view was unreasonable but you didn't say anything.

    (d) It ended in an argument.

3 Last time either of you became heated when discussing a personal issue relevant to your relationship:

    (a) You were able to suspend the discussion sensibly for another time.

    (b) You both continued the argument to the point where you were extremely frustrated and the whole conversation appeared to go nowhere.

    (c) You or your partner became upset and in frustration walked out on the other person.

    (d) You and your partner continued arguing to the point of no return. You were unable to resume any positive interactions for a number of days.

4 Last time you tried to solve a problem in your relationship:

    (a) You were both able, with as little hassle as possible, to reach a mutually satisfactory agreement.

    (b) You wanted to solve the problem your way and did not want to try a solution your partner had suggested.

    (c) Your partner took over the whole show and implemented his/her solution.

    (d) Neither of you reached an agreement and the situation was left up in the air.

5 Last time you both agreed to change in certain ways for the betterment of your relationship:

    (a) You both successfully changed in the agreed way.

    (b) You changed but your partner did not.

    (c) Your partner changed but you did not.

    (d) Neither of you changed; you both forgot about it.

You can use your answers to these questions as a personal guide to what you need to enhance or change in your relationship. If you feel that your answers indicate that you need to change aspects of your behaviour, then the rest of this book should be helpful.

1
Myths and facts about relationships

If the little green men out there really have nothing better to do in their flying saucers than monitor our radio and television transmissions, they must have unavoidably concluded that this planet is inhabited by a not very intelligent species permanently besotted by a peculiar emotion called 'love'.

Any interstellar observer of our popular music, literature, films, theatre or art must be struck by the massive amount of air-time we devote to the experience of 'falling in love'. At the same time it seems paradoxically to be the source of our greatest pleasure, the object of our most desperate endeavours, and the cause of our deepest misery.

Well, like all caricatures, there is a core of truth in our popular representations of love. It **does** feel good to be in love; it **is** exciting to fall in love. It **is** sad when love dies. It is not unreasonable to be interested in love.

And most of us are. The problem is that our interest is met by a lack of factual information or guidance and a plethora of fairy tales. Few of us get a sex education, even today. But almost no-one gets a love education, in any formal or helpful sense. Most of us have three sources of information about love; the example of our parents' relationship, which may or may not be helpful; true romance comics and their various Hollywood kin, which are definitely misleading; and the lies and exaggerations we share with our adolescent peers, which serve only to entrench the myths of Hollywood.

Our steadily climbing divorce rate is concrete evidence of how ill-prepared many of us are for establishing and maintaining successful adult love relationships. Divorce can

Romantic Confessions

be a realistic decision for a couple who genuinely cannot make their relationship work well for both, and it does not have to be harmful to those involved, despite the fact that Australians presently divorce so clumsily that it often is hurtful to all involved, adults and children.

Yet, it is our belief that many divorces and a great deal of heartbreak could be avoided if more people approached their love relationships with realistic expectations and attitudes. Research into the role of expectations and attitudes in marital success or failure shows that most of us believe one or some of eleven myths about adult relationships. Our belief in these myths makes our relationships vulnerable to distress. An important part of effective marital or relationship therapy is to help couples recognise how they have been handicapped by these popular beliefs, how to challenge them, and how to replace them with a realistic view of successful relationships.

When we asked distressed and non-distressed couples how much they believed the marital relationship myths, there was no difference between the two groups. But when we asked distressed couples to describe their relationships, it was obvious that they lived according to the myths, even though they could not see or would not say that they did.

So don't read what follows with too much smugness and self-congratulation for not being so silly as to believe these myths. You might find it illuminating and helpful instead to ask yourself the question, 'How much have I, and my relationships, been unconsciously influenced by these beliefs?'

Relationship Myth Number 1

'If you feel you only like your partner now, that means you have fallen out of love.'

At the end of the movie, the hero rides off into the west, with the heroine romantically wrapped in his arms, each gazing longingly into the other's eyes. We never get to see what happens when they get over the hill.

Many people eventually become disappointed in their relationships because they no longer feel 'in love' the way they used to. Often they will worry about what's wrong with them, or their partner, or the relationship, that they should fall 'out of love' like this. It's not that they don't like each other any more – there may well be a strong mutual liking – but they believe they should feel more than just liking.

The truth is that there are two kinds of love in adult relationships. The first kind, the one presented almost exclusively by Hollywood *et al.*, is called passionate love. It is marked by strong feelings, heart thumpings, tummy turning over, longing for your beloved, in whom you can see only good. Typically you think about each other a lot, especially when apart. Passionate love usually has a strong sexual component and any related sexual activity has the added excitement of novelty.

Passionate love can be very enjoyable, and good, clean fun, with only one problem that unfortunately Hollywood never told you about: it lasts for six to thirty months.

That's what we said. If you put lots of obstacles in its path, you can stretch passionate love out to thirty months. If you move in with each other (or get married) in the heat of the moment, it can be over in six months. Romantics don't like it, and some defensive people have hotly denied it, but that's what the research shows: passionate love is a time-limited phenomenon.

The second kind of love is called companionate love. This is a different kind of feeling, quieter, deeper and more of a strong liking for each other. While it may not have the extreme highs or lows of passionate love, it can be a very emotionally satisfying experience. The sexual relationship may lack the novelty effect of discovering a new partner, but can gain from the partners' knowing and accepting each other and thus feeling comfortable to expand their sexual repertoire.

Initially many people mistakenly see companionate love as a lesser experience than passionate love, instead of realising that they are just different. Passionate love must end, for everybody. Companionate love can last for a lifetime, if you look after it, and is therefore the only love you can base a life-long relationship on.

We shudder to think how many relationships have been needlessly chucked in because one or both partners thinks he or she has fallen out of love. It is not unusual to see young adults wandering through a sequence of six to thirty month relationships, each time saying, 'This is the real thing'. And eventually wondering what's wrong with them because they can't stay 'in love'. It's even sadder that so many of them get married and have kids during the process, leaving broken homes and hearts behind.

Example 1
Sarah and Peter had been married for twelve months. They had been living together for six months before they were married. Their courtship was the typical whirlwind affair.

They met when they were introduced by friends. Peter was

attracted to Sarah's outgoing behaviour whereas he was fairly retiring. Sarah was attracted to Peter's quietness and sensibility.

They both got on really well. They discovered that they had similar interests in music, food and sport. They enjoyed sharing these activities with each other. Their sexual relationship was very exciting for both of them. Both felt they had met the ideal person.

In a flurry of excitement they moved in with each other. Because they were both working, they didn't spend much time together but still spent evenings and weekends going out.

Around six months later they decided that marriage was a good idea. Their relationship remained on a peak, despite occasional ups and downs, and wedding plans involved them in a happy family atmosphere.

A month after they were married Sarah discovered she was pregnant. They were both uncertain about having a child at this stage as financially they were scraping to save for a house. Sarah decided that she would like to have the child, and Peter agreed it would work out.

The financial demands and the demands of the child put a great strain on the relationship. Peter and Sarah spent even less time together. When they did do anything together, it always involved the baby. They stopped going out, in an attempt to save money. Sarah spent most of her day at home, while Peter went off to work.

They began having more frequent disagreements, particularly when they were both tired and irritable.

Sarah started having serious doubts about the relationship. She began wondering if she loved Peter any more. She liked him and at times they got on well together but she felt differently about him. She realised that the strain of saving and looking after the baby affected them both but she thought if their relationship was good they should be able to cope.

She began longing for earlier days and began to withdraw more and more from the relationship. Sex became increasingly dissatisfying for both of them. This made Sarah question how she felt about Peter even more.

It's true that many separating couples don't feel love for each other any more. But that's more because no-one told them how to, rather than because they can't. Companionate love needs perpetual tending. You must keep refreshing your partner's rewardingness for you if you want to stay in love.

The behaviour which does this is called **coupling**: doing good things together as a couple; not independently, not with the family or friends, but just as a couple. Recreational activities alone, as a family, and with other adult friends are important to develop and maintain a network of friendships and a rich rewarding life. But doing some enjoyable things together just as a couple is essential if you are to stay in love (see Chapters 2 and 4).

The top four reasons cited by divorcing Australian couples for the failure of their marriages were all aspects of neglected coupling. Typically Australian couples couple furiously while they are dating or courting. But once the relationship is established, coupling fades away before family, work and friends. And then they wonder why they don't enjoy being with each other anymore.

Sarah and Peter might have approached their marriage differently.

Example 2
Before marrying they both discussed their expectations of marriage, recognising the fact that their passionate feelings towards each other would change but that they had a good basis and enough common interests to make the relationship work.

After they were married they took steps to make sure that they spent enjoyable times together. And they planned for all the responsibilities that would also need to be dealt with.

Once a week, they would leave the baby with one of their mothers and go out together alone. Usually they went to cheap restaurants. When they got home they made love. The next morning they were able to sleep in before picking up the baby. Everyone benefited from this situation. They both looked forward to spending the time together and both grandmothers were delighted to look after the baby.

At times when Sarah was annoyed with something Peter had done or they were coping with a particularly stressful period, she felt less interested in the relationship but she recognised this as a normal process and wasn't worried about these feelings. Generally she liked Peter and was happy to be in the relationship.

Relationship Myth Number 2

'If you and your partner really love each other, you will spend all your time together.'

This myth is the equally illogical converse of the first and is the underlying premise in over-dependent relationships. It is based on the belief that one person can fulfil all the needs – intellectual, social, emotional, recreational, sexual, companionable – of another. Well, somewhere in the world there may be such an ideally complementary couple, but we haven't met them yet.

Each of us has a wide range of needs, which allow us to lead individually rewarding and fulfilling lives. A good relationship meets some of these needs, for each of the partners, some of the time. But it also encourages both of the partners to fulfil their other needs outside of the relationship.

Example 1
Martha and John had been married for five years. During that time they had always done everything together. Everyone said they were an ideal couple.

However things weren't as rosy as they appeared. Martha and John were beginning to have more and more arguments over the time spent together and the time spent apart.

Despite John's disapproval Martha had just begun working part-time. This gave Martha a new sense of freedom. She had even begun thinking of returning to night school to study. John was jealous of any time Martha spent away from him and this was causing conflict.

John wanted Martha at home to look after him; he didn't want her cavorting around with other people and taking time out from being with him.

On the other hand, Martha was enjoying her new life. She no longer wanted always to be with John. With the way he was behaving, however, she felt guilty because she believed she should be home with him. She therefore began to make promises she couldn't keep and let John down even more.

As time progressed, Martha felt more and more resentful of John's behaviour. She began staying out more and more to avoid the conflict.

Clinging to this myth is usually an expression of personal insecurity (see Myths 9 and 10 below), and results in over-possessiveness. This can lead to both feeling trapped in the relationship, smothered by each other, and resentful at the loss of other activities and relationships.

John and Martha were falling into this trap; they might have handled the situation very differently.

Example 2

When Martha announced that she would like to go to work, John and Martha sat down and discussed their expectations of each other.

Even though John may not have been entirely happy with Martha's decision, he recognised that it is important that people explore their own potential and he encouraged Martha to do that.

They also worked out how much time they would both agree to spend together.

Martha and John agreed that she would spend two nights a week on her study course, while John would go out with friends from work on those same two nights. They would spend the rest of their time together, either alone or with friends.

Relationship Myth Number 3

'If you and your partner really love each other, you will automatically know how each other thinks and feels.'

It seems that all couples mind-read (not just psychologists). They feel that, because they have been together or lived together for so long, each knows how the other thinks and feels, without ever listening or asking. This becomes particularly apparent when they argue. Both are so busy preparing their next verbal salvo inside their head that neither has time to listen to what the other actually said.

After living with someone for some length of time, you may sometimes be able to guess what the other person thinks, or because of their non-verbal behaviour you may guess what they feel. But it is a trap to believe that because you sometimes guess right that that means you will **always** know how your partner thinks or feels.

Each of us is responsible for our own thoughts and feelings. You may think that other people are not being truthful about their thoughts or feelings, but how are you really going to know? You can't get inside their head and tell what they are thinking. We all have to accept on trust that what someone says is what they mean. We can't prove otherwise. And trying to prove otherwise will usually only make the other person defensive and lead to an argument.

American research confirms that both distressed and non-distressed couples mind-read, but with one important difference. The partners in a distressed relationship are inclined to assume of each other the meanest possible

motives, the foulest intent, and a general intention to be hurtful and obstructive. Yet the same research found that the two groups did not differ in their intent; the negative impact of interactions in the distressed couples resulted from their interpretations and expectations of each other.

Mind-reading may be inevitable, but if it's negative with no communication to correct it, it can be destructive.

Example 1
Rob and Jill had been married for ten years. Both felt that they had a good relationship overall, although they had some really rough patches at times – usually when they tried to discuss problem issues.

When Rob became upset with Jill, he began to think that Jill wasn't interested in him or the relationship. He accused her of this a couple of times, particularly when she appeared annoyed with him. He said he could tell by the look on her face how she felt. Jill would hotly deny these accusations, thinking to herself that because Rob was so upset he must have found something wrong with her. She would tell Rob that he was just being stubborn and she knew he really was saying that because he wanted to leave her. They would pass these accusations back and forth between each other until the argument developed into one almighty row.

This was undermining their good feelings about each other.

Rob and Jill could have handled the situation differently.

Example 2
Every time they discussed a problem, they sat down quietly together and used their communication skills. Because they were listening carefully to each other and responding to the other's message without making their own interpretations, they were able to discuss problems without getting into so much difficulty.

Their conversation went something like this:

Rob: 'When you look so uncertain when I ask if you would like to go out with me, I feel upset.'

Jill: 'I can understand how that would upset you. I am sorry, I was actually thinking that you looked uncertain about asking me out.'

They were both able at least to discuss their uncertainties.

Relationship Myth Number 4

'If you and your partner really love each other, you will automatically communicate well.'

At first glance, this myth looks like the last, but there is an important difference. Couples under the influence of Myth No. 3 don't even try to communicate, because they don't think they need to.

The effect of Myth No. 4 is to believe that good communication comes 'naturally', without learning, practice or effort. Many couples coming to therapy tell us they communicate well, and undoubtedly sincerely believe that they do. But even a brief observation of their interactions shows that one or both may be bottling up feelings, denying the other's feelings or opinions, or being aggressive or defensive.

Ian and Cecilia had been married for two years. They felt they were happy and they had a good relationship but they couldn't understand why they had sudden fighting outbursts over trivial issues.

Neither Cecilia nor Ian would say anything to each other if either of them felt upset. Cecilia believed that Ian should 'know' she was upset so she didn't say anything. Ian believed that it wasn't worth upsetting Cecilia by saying anything, besides she knew how he felt by the way he behaved.

After two years of living together and two years of marriage there were a number of problem situations that occurred between them but they were so worried about hurting each other and causing more arguments that they didn't say anything at the time. On the other hand, at times little issues would blow up into arguments.

Cecilia and Ian were bottling up feelings by not saying

anything, then a little event would trigger these bad feelings off and they would rush out in a torrent.

They both believed that their partner should know how they felt without them saying anything, but then they felt resentful when the other person didn't notice how they felt.

This was causing more and more bad feelings which was influencing other enjoyable aspects of their relationship.

There are three basic skills in good communication: levelling (telling your partner how you feel), listening (**not** mind-reading), and validating (accepting your partner's opinions and feelings, even when they're different from your own). Like all complex skills, you need the chance to learn them, a chance which unfortunately few of us get (see Chapter 3).

Relationship Myth Number 5

'If the relationship is in trouble, usually one of the partners is to blame (usually the other partner).'

When distressed couples come to therapy, they will usually explain the difficulty in their relationship as due to personal faults in each other. 'If he wasn't so selfish, Doc', and 'If she wasn't so immature, Doc', then everything would be fine.

This character-assassination harks back to the old-fashioned view of relationship success as depending on the compatibility of the 'personalities' of the two partners. It's a notion that is perpetuated by organisations that claim to find you a suitable partner by matching your personal character-istics with those of potential mates. The whole idea is hogwash.

Research over the last twenty years casts serious doubt on the idea that people have stable, measurable 'personalities' at all. And the marital therapy based on this approach, which focussed on 'curing' the 'sick' partner, was marked by a singular lack of success.

If it were true that your relationship was in strife because you had married a selfish, inconsiderate bastard, then more fool you for making such a stupid choice. The trouble with character-assassination is that it is a dead-end: once you have labelled your partner as personally deficient, you have nowhere else to go but out of the relationship.

As a result of this research, relationship therapy changed to focus on the two people, and the interaction between them. It concentrated on teaching them skills of interacting, and was more successful than relying merely on assessing the personalities of the two people – apart from cases where one of the partners had a severe psychological problem such as alcoholism. But therapists using this approach found that some couples could practise their relationship skills under their supervision in a clinic, but didn't seem to be able to apply them at home – they made no real progress in therapy and usually eventually split up.

Certainly relationship success depends on the relationship skills used by the couple, but we stress that there is one more vital ingredient in a successful relationship: the self-talk of each of the partners.

One of the handicapping attitudes forced on us as children is the idea that there is something wrong with loving yourself. Many parents and teachers are stinting with praise and approval because they don't want their children to get swelled heads, and they would sincerely like the kids to do well. But what a child learns in this praise-deficient environment is that he or she should always do better, and has never done quite well enough.

If you don't see yourself as lovable – as reasonably attractive, interesting, likeable and sexy – then you won't believe it when your partner says, 'I love you'. Your self-talk will be: 'I wonder what he/she wants this time, because I know he/she can't mean that, because I know no-one could really love me.'

These personally insecure people put their partners through perpetual tests of love, always seeking more proof of something which they themselves are basically unwilling to accept. They are the partners most threatened by outside interests and most jealous of other relationships. In the end, they usually drive their partners up the wall and out of the relationship. When a distressed couple start to assassinate each other's characters, we now tell them that almost certainly both are contributing to the difficulties in the relationship, and both must be willing to change some of the things they do and some of the things they think, if the relationship is to improve.

But we also take care to screen each of the partners individually for their self-esteem, particularly in the context of intimate relationships. You must first be able to love yourself before you can successfully love someone else.

You need to do the same screening process for your relationship. Does one of you seriously lack self-confidence? Do you believe that you are reasonably attractive, interesting and sexy?

If individual self-esteem is a problem for one or both of you, this manual won't help with that. If you want to tackle self-esteem problems by a self-help programme, we have suggested a couple in Chapter 9.

But you should recognise that this means your situation is more complicated, and you might be better off seeing a clinically qualified psychologist.

Relationship Myth Number 6

'If you and your partner love each other, good sex comes naturally.'

We are getting fed up with 'naturalness freaks'. It was 'natural' for most humans to die before they were one year old for most of our history but no-one seems to want to reinstate that part of natural existence. Nowadays, about all that comes 'naturally' to humans is crying in babies and halitosis in adults.

Some animals inherit patterns of behaviour wired into their system from birth. For example, chickens from the day they hatch will always peck at round objects, and most animals have pre-set patterns of mating behaviour. Unlike these animals we have very few inherited patterns of behaviour. We abandoned that advantage and instead our behaviour is learned, to cope with a greater range and change of environment. This is what we call 'intelligence'.

One cost of this greater intelligence is that each of us has to learn from scratch even basic behaviours which seem to come automatically in simpler species. What you lose on the swings, you gain on the roundabouts. An oyster may lead a naively content existence but he doesn't get to travel much.

Few people expect complicated skills to come 'naturally'. We learn to drive, to cook, to ski, even to play games. Sexual expression involves a variety of movements, usually inter-acting in a complex way with another person's responses.

There is no logical reason to expect these skills to come any more 'naturally' than others, particularly not when you consider the number of distorting influences acting on them.

Our sex education from birth onwards is very poor, from non-existent to downright lies. Children are told not to talk about sex, so they learn to talk about it behind their parents' backs, and get all sorts of inaccurate information from their peers. Even if you did get a sex education it was usually about reproduction, nothing is ever mentioned about having sex for fun, or pleasure, and there is no mention of human relations.

It is a wonder we don't see more people with sexual problems. And most of the sexual problems that we do see have initially stemmed from inaccurate knowledge with no chance to learn the necessary skills for a satisfactory sexual relationship.

One of the outstanding examples of this process in our society is that a large majority of women have not experienced orgasm before they enter a sexual relationship because of taboos on masturbation and the associated guilt if the woman attempts to masturbate. The woman therefore has no idea of how to experience an orgasm within the context of a sexual relationship and this can often lead to dissatisfaction with associated doubts about the whole relationship.

Example 1
Anne's marriage was okay, although there was some tension over her dissatisfaction with the sexual relationship. She enjoyed sex, at first, but gradually found it less satisfactory. She had had three other sexual relationships before meeting her husband; she always enjoyed sex, but now doesn't think she ever climaxed.

Anne was beginning to doubt her feelings for her husband. She thought that if they both cared for each other they should have a good sexual relationship. Her dissatisfaction crystallised a year ago when she read an article about female sexuality. She tried masturbating then, although she had not masturbated before ('I didn't think of girls doing it') – but gave up after five minutes because: 'I didn't feel anything'.

She was beginning to feel more resentful that her husband didn't know how to help her, her doctor and a gynaecologist weren't able to help either. Anne's husband also began to feel guilty because he thought that there was something wrong with their marriage if Anne wasn't satisfied sexually. She wondered if she really 'loved' her husband and began to have doubts about the relationship.

Both Anne and her husband tended to avoid sex because they felt so badly about it, and this affected other aspects of their relationship.

A good sexual relationship grows from two partners having realistic expectations, each comfortable with his or her own sexuality, learning and accepting more about themselves and each other, through open communication (see Chapter 4).

Example 2
Anne and her husband could have approached this situation differently (of course with a good human relations education they may never have had the problem).

Anne could have told her husband as early as possible that she was feeling more and more dissatisfied with their sexual relationship. Although both of them may feel upset about this situation, they could be supportive of each other and recognise that despite the problem it need not affect how they feel about their relationship, as long as they do something constructive to change the situation.

Relationship Myth Number 7

'Arguments clear the air, and enable you to make up and feel good.'

This silly notion has been pushed in some of the pop psychology junkbooks, with titles like *How to Fight Dirty and Stab Your Partner in the Back*. The idea seems to be that it is useful to 'let off steam' and vent your bad feelings towards your partner.

It is certainly not a good idea to bottle up feelings, good or bad, and you should share these with your partner, but by talking and listening to each other not by fighting. Fighting in relationships serves only one purpose: it is destructive.

When couples argue, they show several characteristic behaviours. They kitchen-sink: throwing everything into the argument but the kitchen sink. They side-track: introducing more and more irrelevant issues. They muck-rake: rehearsing all of the other person's past misdeeds and mistakes. They self-listen: each attending only to what he or she is saying or wants to say. And they character-assassinate: saying exaggerated, over-generalised and hurtful things about each other.

An example of a couple arguing

'I saw you flirting with Julie last night. Anyone would think you were a prize Casanova.' (aggressive opening statement)

'What do you mean? You have rocks in your head.' (character-assassination)

'Everyone saw you and her huddled in the corner, giggling and laughing. You were just out to pay me back.' (mind-reading)

'You are an old nagger. Every time we go to a party you nag me about who I spoke to. I am fed up with you.' (character-assassination, over-generalisation)

'Me nag? Well if you did what you were meant to I would not have to nag. Like last night when I asked you to put out the garbage. You deliberately ignored me.' (sidetracking, muckraking, mind-reading)

'Here you go again, always accusing me of wrongs. What about you when you got pissed to the eyeballs at that party last year and I just about had to drag you off that fellow, what's-is-name. Fine example you were. You can't talk.' (character-assassination, muckraking, sidetracking)

'Well what about your office party? You were a disgrace. I am sick and tired of your behaviour in public. I feel like staying home rather than going out. Besides you're always out with your mates. You never take me anywhere decent, and then when we go out you flirt with everything in a skirt.' (muckraking, self-listening, sidetracking, kitchen-sinking)

Guess what the outcome of this argument will be. They are hardly going to feel good; they may eventually feel relieved when things return to normal, but they are not going to feel good after the argument.

Later, you can say you are sorry (and mean it) and that you didn't really mean all of the hurtful things you said (and be sincere), but you can't take them back, nor easily wipe away their effects. Arguments chip away at the good faith in a relationship, at each partner's ability to believe the other's statements of love. Keep fighting, and eventually you pass a point of no return for the relationship, beyond which neither partner is willing to trust the other emotionally again (see Chapters 3 and 5).

The couple in the above example could have dealt with the situation in the following way.

Ideally they should have discussed their past grievances at the time so there was no need to bring them up again. Even if they hadn't discussed them they would have to put them aside at this point.

'I found it disturbing last night when you paid so much attention to Julie.'

'I am sorry you were upset. I didn't mean to do that. Julie and I get on well together and I enjoy talking to her.'

'But what about how I feel?'

'Hey, I know you feel upset, and we need to sit down and work this problem out but I would rather do that when we can both talk calmly.'

'Yes, that's true. I am upset and I don't want to argue. Give me a couple of hours to calm down. How about we talk about this before lunch?'

'Good idea.'

Relationship Myth Number 8

'An argument can only end by one partner giving in and admitting that he or she is wrong.'

This is the myth that keeps arguments going on . . . and on . . . and on. Both partners become increasingly upset, and each can only see how right 'I' am, and how stubborn 'he' or 'she' is for not admitting they are wrong.

Of course sometimes one of them is wrong, because some arguments are over factual matters, like when the local bank opens. The argument could be settled by finding out the facts for yourself, like ringing the bank and asking what their hours are. But even when a difference of opinion is over a factual matter, arguing is the worst way of trying to settle it.

Shouting at your partner is the best way of making him or her defensive, and all the more likely to dig in his or her toes, even if the facts are reasonably clear.

Example
Loud angry voice: 'Would you pick up your clothes.'
Response, angrily: 'No, why should I?'

as against:

Level voice: 'I feel angry when clothes are left on the floor. Would you pick them up please?'
Level tone: 'Yes, I know I keep forgetting. I will have to think of something that will jog my memory each time.'

In any case, most arguments in relationships are not over factual matters, but over differences of opinion, feelings or experiences.

It may be perfectly true for him to say, 'I love skiing'. It may be equally true for her to say, 'I hate skiing'. For each of them, their statements are true even though they are different. It's amazing how many couples will conduct World War III each trying to convince the other to abandon his or her feelings in favour of the other's way of looking at things.

It is not necessary for a successful relationship that both partners have exactly the same ideas, opinions, preferences, reactions, and so on. It *is* necessary that they accept each other's individuality and right to feel and think differently. Much needless fighting and hurt could be averted by simply saying to each other, 'Yes, I can see that's how it is for you. It's not how I feel, but I accept that it's how you feel.'

Often this simple recognition and acceptance of differences is all that is necessary. Sometimes it means that the couple have identified an important difference in values or goals or whatever. Then they need to use problem-solving skills to negotiate a resolution that suits both of them.

Antiquated marriage counselling often urged couples to resolve differences by compromise. A compromise is a no-win solution, a decision that falls somewhere between what both partners wanted, satisfying neither. Problem-solving involves brainstorming new solutions to the problem until one is found that suits both partners. It is the win-win solution when both partners feel that their opinions have been taken into account in important decisions (see Chapter 6).

Relationship Myth Number 9

'If your partner feels love for someone else, she/he must feel less love for you.'

This myth is based on the pie theory of love. According to this theory, somewhere inside us, presumably in the heart region, we have a fixed amount of love to dole out, like a pie. If you give a slice of your love pie to someone other than your partner, then there must be less left for you to give your partner. So your partner should feel threatened and jealous.

There is no evidence to support a pie theory of love. In fact, the opposite seems true. The more a person is able to experience successful love relationships, the more he or she will be able to express love. Most of us have a number of love relationships at once: with our children, our parents, our spouses, our special friends.

Jealousy towards a partner feeling love towards another adult of similar age and sex as ourselves is really an expression of our own insecurity and lack of self-confidence. Basically, the jealous partner is thinking: 'I can't possibly stand any competition, because I am so ugly, uninteresting and boring in bed that my partner is certain to find someone else more attractive.' Added to this self-devaluation is often the further thought that, 'If I lose this relationship I cannot possibly find another one.'

One insecure partner may value jealous responses in another in a desperate attempt to bolster his or her own low self-esteem: 'He must really love me to be that jealous'. But to most of us, jealous behaviour is a pain in the neck. Being interrogated, snooped on, and required to account for every minute and movement will drive most of us up the wall and out of the relationship.

In contrast, feeling free to have feelings of love for any number of people can make a person more attracted to, and happy in, her relationship. How, and to what extent, those feelings are expressed needs to be subject to negotiation and mutual agreement, but having them ought not disturb anyone or threaten any relationship.

Relationship Myth Number 10

'If your partner feels sexually attracted to someone else, she/he must feel less attracted to you.'

This is the sexual version of the pie theory: you are supposed only to have a fixed amount of sexual attraction, so if you are giving some to someone other than your partner, you must have less left for your partner. So your partner should feel hurt and jealous.

We have lost track of the number of people who have insisted to us that jealousy is 'natural'. We hope by now that our views on 'naturalness' are clear. Cross-cultural research has shown that what we are jealous of is what we have been taught to feel jealous of.

In the South Pacific cultures, before they were influenced by the missionaries, sex was not a source of jealousy as it is for us. If a man and woman met in the bush by chance, and felt so inclined, then they 'naturally' had sex, and no-one batted an eyelid. But if they were to eat together that would have caused a storm. Eating together, in that culture, had some of the connotations that our culture gives sex.

Our culture teaches jealousy based on pride, possessiveness and insecurity. If your partner loves or has sex with someone else, that is supposed to represent a devaluing of you. After all, you own your partner's body and feelings – what right has he to use them other than as you direct. Besides if she has sex with someone else, she will discover how really boring you are.

Most of us are sexually attracted to a number of people at different times, although most of us choose not to act on those feelings most of the time, which is probably just as well or the world might be quite chaotic. We can acknowledge the feelings, but exercise some reasonable self-control over their expression.

Two people with a very good, long-standing sexual relationship may experience sexual attraction for others without any diminution in their attraction for each other. Indeed, sexual success is likely to foster a healthier level of sexual interest. Again, how and to what extent they express their respective sexual feelings outside their relationship needs to be subject to negotiation and mutual agreement.

Some couples only feel happy expecting total sexual fidelity of each other. Some seem to be comfortable in open sexual sharing, such as swinging. The content of each couple's agreement about expectations of outside sexual involvements is not as important as the fact that there needs to be such an agreement, as explicit as possible.

A sensible discussion and agreement on the rules for involvement in outside relationships would save a lot of unnecessary hurt and deception. We see couples come to therapy time after time, where the precipitating factor is the distress caused by one of the partners becoming involved in an outside relationship. We are not saying this is the cause of the distressed marriage but it adds further hurt and upset to the already distressed relationship.

Most Australian relationships begin with romantic expectations based on the myths we are debunking here. It is usually implicitly assumed that a long-term relationship will be sexually monogamous and this assumption is typically only discussed when it has already been broken by one of the partners. The heat and steam of such discussions is rarely conducive to any realistic consideration of mutual expectations.

We have rarely seen people cope with more than one long-term relationship at the same time but the threat of more casual relationships is usually exaggerated. We have never seen a person leave a successful relationship because he or she has become involved in an alternative relationship. We have seen people seek alternative relationships because their long-term relationships were already unsatisfactory.

As a rule of thumb, what determines the success and the future of a relationship is what the two partners do, or do not do, between them. It is not determined by what one or the other partner may do outside the relationship.

Relationship Myth Number 11

'If you want your partner to do something, nagging is the best way to get him or her to do it. If you want your partner to stop nagging, give in to it.'

This myth looks so silly in black and white that no-one will ever admit to believing it. But it's amazing how many couples run their relationships as if the myth were true. Nagging can be more subtle than just a repetitive whinge. Silent sulking and suffering martyrdom are both forms of nagging, in the sense of being attempts to coerce your partner into doing what you want in return for your turning off an unpleasant behaviour.

Nagging, defined in those terms, represents the breakdown of open communication and the absence of problem-solving negotiation skills. It is characteristic of distressed relationships that the partners gradually exchange more and more unpleasant behaviours in increasingly hostile attempts to control each other's behaviour (and feelings). Such a pattern can, of course, have only one outcome, unless they do get the chance to acquire some communication and problem-solving skills.

AN ALTERNATIVE VIEW OF RELATIONSHIPS

If you set out to drive across the Nullarbor Desert in a clapped out 1941 jeep running on only three cylinders, it's unlikely you'd get to the other side. Your expectations would be unrealistic.

If you go into relationships with unrealistic expectations, you are equally unlikely to be successful. In marital therapy we invariably spend some time challenging the unrealistic expectations spelled out in the myths we have discussed. In our view, a prerequisite for success in love relationships is to embark with realistic expectations of what you can and cannot get from them, and of what you need to do to make them work.

In place of the myths, we suggest to couples the following view of relationships as a basis for them to work out their expectations of each other and the relationship. Sometimes we are accused of putting forward an unattainable ideal, but we disagree. The end result of thinking and working on your relationship is not that you have a perfect relationship – who does? – but that you have the knowledge and skills to keep making your relationship as good as it can be for both of you, now, and as each of you and therefore your relationship change in the future.

A good relationship provides some, but not all, of each partner's needs. They do some enjoyable things together as a couple, and they also value each other's independent activities. There is clear and prompt communication of feelings when that's important, accompanied by active listening. Important decision-making is shared. Important differences are resolved by calm problem solving and negotiation to find mutually acceptable solutions. They share a mutually satisfactory and enjoyable sexual relationship. Each of the partners feels reasonably free to have feelings for and relationships with other people, but both choose to do this in agreed ways. And each of the partners feels reasonably free to be him or herself.

PRACTICAL EXERCISE

Discuss relationship myths

After you have both read this chapter, set aside time to think about what it means to your relationship.

Do you agree with any of these myths?

Do other couples you know live as though these myths are true?

Did your parents live as though these myths were true?

How much do you think these myths have influenced your behaviour?

Which myths do you need to change for yourself?

Discuss these questions with your partner after you have both read the myths.

How much has your relationship been influenced by popular myths?

What do you expect of and in your relationship in the future?

Be as concrete and specific as possible. If you identify points for which you have importantly different expectations, write them down, and suspend them until you've done Chapters 6 and 7.

2
Making relationships more rewarding: coupling

A successful relationship is one you enjoy being in. It's a rewarding place to be. Staying in a relationship as an obligation or duty, or because you are too frightened to go it alone is typically a recipe for depression, resentment and unhappiness for all involved. If your motivation for being in your relationship is obligation or fear, and you can't change that, perhaps you should be working on Chapter 9.

But the absence of problems, if you achieve that through this programme, could leave you with just a neutral experience in your relationship, not a rewarding one. Which is why this chapter is important. Much of the advice in other chapters is aimed at helping you to solve or prevent problems. That could leave you with the neutral experience, possibly an improvement over negative feelings, but not much to spend your life in.

This chapter and Chapter 4 are aimed at helping you to make your relationship more rewarding, to increase the positive feelings you have in it and about your partner. For many couples, this will be the most important part of improving their relationships.

In a recent Australian survey of divorcing couples, the top three reasons given for breaking up their marriages were all problems in this area: 45 per cent cited 'sexual incompatibility' as a cause of their break-up (see Chapter 4); 40 per cent cited a 'lack of common interests'; and 40 per cent complained that the husband was not home enough. Some couples, of course, gave more than one reason.

Most of us would like to think that we go into, and stay in,

WIZARD OF ID

our relationships for love. Although other research has shown that quite often we actually go into our relationships for reasons other than love, it is still not unreasonable to expect to develop and share companionate love in a successful long-term relationship.

Feelings, including love, do not just happen. They are the results of what happens to us, what we do, and how we think about all of this. Later in this chapter we'll systematically look at how you can change your thoughts in this area. What happens to us is partly determined by what we do, so now we will concentrate on changing what you do in order to make your relationship more rewarding and to generate feelings of love.

COUPLING

We call doing good things together, as a couple, coupling. In a balanced life, you will each have some recreational activities that you do independently of each other, some that you share with your family and some with friends. But for the sake of your relationship you will also have some that you do as a couple, excluding all others. This is coupling.

Coupling seems to be the most commonly neglected area of Australian relationships (see the divorce statistics above). Usually people spend a lot of time doing pleasant activities together early in the relationship. But once they are married or established in living together, these activities seem to dwindle.

The everyday tasks of managing a home, looking after children, or coping with jobs gradually occupy more of the couple's time. Many couples eventually do little or no coupling. Some of the couples coming to us for therapy cannot remember when they had their last date as a couple.

If this lack of coupling continues for any length of time, both partners tend to find the relationship and each other less attractive or interesting. They become what has been called 'intimate strangers', drifting further and further apart emotionally.

Coupling is essential if you are to stay in love and to feel that you want to stay in your relationship because it is enjoyable and rewarding. If you do not see much of your partner, or if, when you do see your partner, it is mostly in association with dull, boring or unrewarding activities, you should not be surprised if you gradually see your partner as dull and boring.

As a relationship becomes established, it is easy to fill your time together with routine activities. Although these activities may be important and may give you some satisfaction from completing them, they are not always enjoyable or rewarding in themselves. It is also possible to do individually enjoyable activities while you are near each other, with very little coupling involved, like watching television.

One or both of you may develop, or redevelop, an independent recreation which takes up a lot of your time. When you add work, and other outside commitments, there may be little or no time left for your coupling.

In Chapter 1 we discussed passionate and companionate love, and made the point that companionate love is the only kind you can expect to base a long-term relationship on, because it is the only one of the two love experiences that can last for more than a few years. Providing you look after it.

However difficult it may be to define love to everybody's satisfaction – and a number of people have tried to debate the ideas of passionate and companionate love with us – we don't think that any love just happens 'naturally'. You have to work on it, in your thoughts and actions.

Love in relationships comes from both partners expressing and showing how much they like each other in their day-to-day interactions, and making the effort to spend time together pursuing enjoyable activities, expressing affection, communicating about good and bad feelings, and resolving problems successfully.

A good sexual relationship is obviously an important part of coupling. It ought not to be the only enjoyable activity the couple share, as unfortunately sometimes happens, but it should be part of their coupling menu. Good sex comes no more 'naturally' than any other complex skill (see Chapter 1), so we have devoted Chapter 4 to practical advice on how to enhance your sexual relationship.

But we want to foreshadow that, and postpone it, for now. You cannot divorce your sexual relationship from the rest of your relationship. If you have been fighting all day, or just ignoring each other, you cannot realistically expect to hop into bed and have a good time together.

One-night stands work, at least in meeting sexual desires for some people, because of the absence of an on-going relationship between the participants. You can't expect to impose one-night stands on an on-going relationship. Successful sexuality in an on-going relationship is more an extension of already shared physical affection and emotional closeness.

In marital therapy, we usually advise couples to wait until the rewardingness of their relationship has improved, and they have mastered reasonable communication skills, before beginning their sexual enhancement programme. In this way, we think, they are giving their sexual enhancement programme its best chance of working well.

The aim of this part of the programme is to introduce to you the steps you will need to take to enhance your coupling skills and organise other time commitments, including other recreational and leisure activities. As with other aspects of this programme, it is desirable that both you and your partner work together to change your relationship. However, you can only take responsibility for your efforts, not your partner's efforts.

So far we have discussed the importance of spending time together, just as a couple, doing pleasant activities. However, coupling need not always be time-consuming or expensive. It is desirable that you and your partner develop a range of coupling activities that vary from lengthy and expensive, to brief and requiring no expense.

Assessing and planning recreational activities

The first step is for you and your partner to work out how much time you spend in different kinds of recreation, as a couple, as a family, as a couple with friends, as a parent with children, and individually. Not all these areas may be relevant for you; leave out those that aren't.

Take a typical week and count the number of hours you spend in leisure or recreation, using the chart below. Get a sheet of paper and draw up your own chart.

Number of hours	Day	Activity	Other(s) present

In the first column write down the number of hours you spent doing the activity, not including the time spent at work or doing everyday household jobs. The activity should be something that you do as a hobby or recreation. It might be at home, or away from home, for example, sewing at home, playing golf, swimming, playing cards. In the Other(s) present column write down if you did the activity by yourself, with your partner, as a couple with friends, with another member of the family, as a family, or with friends.

Below is an example of how your record might look.

Number of hours	Day	Activity	Other(s) present
1	Mon.	Swimming	Self, friends
2	Tues.	Reading	Self, son
3	Wed.	Dinner	Partner, friends
4	Fri.	Drive-in	Family
2	Sat.	Tennis	Self, daughter
3	Sat.	Dinner	Partner, family
4	Sun.	Picnic	Family

In this example the time the person spent with friends alone, with friends with her partner, with her family, and with her children is very good. All of those relationships are probably satisfying and enjoyable. However, in the week she and her partner have never spent any time together just as a couple. They spend time together with friends or family, and this is important, but it is also important, if they want to maintain a successful love relationship, that they do pleasant and enjoyable activities together as a couple.

If you and your partner discover that you are in a similar position to the couple in this example, then you need to follow the suggestions below. If you and your partner are already doing pleasant activities together, then you may find the following suggestions enhance your coupling and other recreational activities.

It is worth mentioning that although we will mainly focus on you and your partner's relationship, because it is our guess that is the area that needs the most work, these suggestions can be applied to all sorts of relationships. For example, it is important that you as a family do pleasant activities together. That you and your partner individually do some things alone with the children. That you and your partner develop some independent interests. And that you as a couple spend time with friends.

PRACTICAL EXERCISE

Increasing coupling activities

Step 1 You and your partner sit down and independently write a list of possible activities you would like to try. At this stage do not worry if your partner would or would not like to do the activities you are writing down. The activities should include a range of choices, from a little time to more time, and ranging in cost from nothing to more expensive activities.

For example, your list may look like this:

going out to dinner
read a book together
have dinner at home by the fire
watch a good movie on TV
go for a picnic
go to the football
spend a weekend in the country
a massage
a hug
learn photography
do some gardening
learn to ski
cook a meal together
go to a film
have a drink together and discuss the day

Step 2 After you have both written out your 'coupling menu' sit down together and read through the lists. Do not be disheartened if at first there appears to be nothing in common. Your 'menu' may look like the above example, but your partner's may look like this:

    play squash
    watch the football
    play cards
    go out to dinner
    go for a walk
    dance
    listen to records
    go swimming
    go camping
    play tennis
    go shopping

At first glance the only common activity for this couple would be 'going to dinner'. However, if you think carefully, there are ways of combining activities. This couple could go camping for a weekend in the country, they could go for a picnic and swim, they could have a massage while listening to records, they could shop for food and then make dinner together, they could go for a walk and take photographs, they could go to dinner and dance afterwards.

There are a large number of possible shared activities, despite no obvious common interests at first glance. As well as combining activities from your coupling menus, either one of you may like to try something the other person mentioned. In this example the couple may both like to learn to ski. Or they may both become interested in becoming good squash players. The partner who did not think of shopping may enjoy doing that as a coupling activity.

There are three rules when deciding upon a coupling activity:

1 Be prepared to try new activities. You may be surprised how much you enjoy it.

2 Be flexible in combining activities. You may both be able to include activities you enjoy, as well as sharing them with your partner.

3 Do not do something you do not like. The idea of coupling is to enjoy yourselves: there is no point in one partner unwillingly doing something that is not enjoyable for him/her. Your partner can always participate in this activity by him/herself.

You and your partner should try to generate a list of ten or more activities that you could try as coupling exercises. If you are having difficulty doing this, check that neither of you is stalling by being unncessarily negative. For example, 'He never wants to do anything I want to do', 'We have nothing in common'. If this is happening, it is important that you:

Check your self-talk or what you are saying to yourself about your partner and your relationship. (This is discussed in more detail at the end of this chapter and more fully in chapter 5. If necessary refer to those sections before continuing here.)

Step 3 Now you are ready to arrange a coupling date. Which activity are you going to try first? When are you going to do it?

Make a date that will allow enough time to prepare. Remember, when you make a date with your partner, it is like any other appointment. Do not break it, unless there is some unforeseen circumstance that makes it really necessary to change your date.

Who will arrange the date? What arrangements will you need to make for the children? Who will be responsible for these arrangements? What happens if for some reason the arrangements you make have to be cancelled, for example, if you decide to go on a picnic and it rains on the day, or if one of the children is sick on the night of your date? Plan ahead for these events and discuss alternative arrangements or times (use your communication skills, when discussing these issues).

Step 4 How will you remember to do some regular coupling?

We recommend to couples that they spend time coupling at least once a week. As we said before, it is important for you and your partner to spend time together as a couple if you are to find your relationship rewarding. Once a week seems a reasonable minimum frequency for coupling, although this may not always be possible.

It is very easy when you are trying to change areas of your relationship to slip back into old habits. It is therefore important, if you are to maintain the changes you have made, to develop ways of making sure that you keep up the new habits. There are a number of ways of making sure you regularly do some coupling. You may decide that it is convenient to set aside a regular time for coupling, for example every Friday and Wednesday evening. Or you may decide that it is better to plan a week or more ahead, so you set aside time on Sunday evenings to discuss coupling plans for the coming week.

Do not leave it to chance for coupling to occur. Both of you need to take responsibility for your relationship and to make sure that you have some strategy that will enable you to remember to keep coupling.

If you are striking difficulties and are unable to establish regular coupling times, once again:

1 Check your self-talk.
2 Check your communication.
3 Check your priorities.

How important is your relationship, compared to other activities you fill your time with? It is true that all of us have limited time, and there are work commitments, commitments to friends, family and individual activities. We have agreed that all of these areas are important if you are to lead a full and satisfying life. However, if you spend time in all these other areas and no time with your partner, you are in danger of letting your relationship become empty and dissatisfying for both of you. If you really believe all these other areas are more important than your relationship, that is your choice, but you should understand the likely consequences of choosing everything else above your relationship.

At the same time it is important that you do not go to the other extreme of cutting yourself and your partner off from enjoyable group, family or individual activities, solely for the sake of your relationship. Both of you would eventually find this also dissatisfying. Striking a balance between all of these recreations is the aim. This may mean at times that you sacrifice individual activities for coupling activities. You may spend less time working, so you can see your family and partner more often. You may develop more independent activities of your own, so that you are not always reliant on your family and partner. These changes in the long run will lead to a better balance of interests and enjoyment in your life.

PRACTICAL EXERCISE
Exchanging pleasure giving in your relationship

It seems that most of us spend a lot of time focussing on the negative aspects of situations. We are quick to recognise and complain about things we do not like, and ignore many of the good things. It is typical of distressed couples to focus totally on the negative aspects of their relationship, and to forget about positive things. When this occurs daily in a relationship, it undermines any of the good that is occurring because, when something good happens, it is not noticed. For example, if you make your partner a nice meal and he does not say anything, then you are less likely to make a special meal again. If this happens over years, you are less likely to try doing anything nice for each other.

Even if your relationship is not distressed, you can probably benefit from enhancing the nice things that exist already.

The idea of this exercise is to get you to focus on the good things in your relationship. Many couples may benefit from a refresher course in giving pleasure in their relationship.

Often when we suggest this to people they complain that there are not many good things to notice. However, when they start looking, they are surprised at what they have taken for granted on the positive side, and what they sometimes overemphasised on the negative side.

Step 1 Your first task is to each keep a diary of acts of 'pleasure giving' for a week. Both get little note-books that you can use as your diaries. Then start noting down all the things your partner does that please you. You will have to become more aware of your partner's pleasing behaviour. This may range from small acts of pleasure giving, such as making you a cup of coffee, to larger acts of pleasure giving like bringing home a surprise present. There can also be things that involve household-type tasks, such as cleaning up the bedroom, or remembering to shop.

Your diary may look like this:

Monday   coffee in bed; made breakfast and helped get the children ready for school; remembered to put out the garbage bin.

Tuesday   nice hug before going to work; baby-sat while I went out; asked me about my day when I got home at night.

Wednesday   tidied up the house; commented on my appearance; made a nice dinner; initiated sex.

Thursday   took the children to school; brought home a box of chocolates; a big hug and kiss; helped make dinner.

Friday   listened to my complaints about work; planned the weekend; brought me a cup of coffee.

Saturday   made a special breakfast; did household tasks together; went out to dinner; made good love together.

Sunday   read paper together; played with children; tidied up the mess; made a nice lunch; left me alone to work on an important project.

Before you continue with this procedure, it is necessary that both you and your partner have recorded your acts of pleasure giving for about a week or more.

Listed below are ten areas in which pleasure giving can occur in relationships. Try to identify some in each area, unless it is irrelevant (e.g. care of children).

FINANCES
HOUSEHOLD MANAGEMENT
CARE OF CHILDREN
MANAGEMENT OF LEISURE TIME
PERSONAL HABITS AND APPEARANCES
SEX
AFFECTION
APPROVAL AND ACCEPTANCE
COMMUNICATION
WORK

Step 2 Find a time to sit down together and swap diaries. At first you may find it easier just to hand your diary to your partner. But after you have done this, practise actually saying to your partner what you found pleasing about her behaviour.

In the above example, the person would say: 'On Monday I liked you bringing me coffee in bed.'

Or, 'Thanks for playing with the kids when I was busy.'

You may both feel strange telling each other what you found pleasing. However this is probably because you are out of practice. It is therefore all the more important that you go through this exercise. No-one ever died of feeling strange.

After you have done this, tell your partner what gave you most pleasure, what pleasure was a complete surprise, and what pleasure was most helpful. You will both be starting to gather information about what your partner finds pleasing and important in your relationship. You may be in for a few surprises.

Repeat the above exercise for as many weeks as you feel is necessary, until both you and your partner begin to feel comfortable telling each other what you find pleasing.

A word of warning: At the moment you will have to put aside your grievances, just concentrate on giving pleasure.

Step 3 The next step is to be able to communicate your awareness of what your partner does that pleases you, at the time he does it.

So you now tell your partner, at least once a day, what he does that pleases you, at the time it happens. You can call this: 'Catch your partner doing something nice'. You are both to be on the look-out for a chance to praise your partner. It is always better to tell someone that you like what they are doing, at the time it happens. This has more impact on them, and increases the likelihood of their repeating the behaviour.

The more you practise saying nice things to each other the more spontaneous this will become. Do not worry if at first your praising feels 'unnatural'; the more you practise the easier it will be.

Step 4 By now you should be more aware of what pleases your partner and able to communicate your own pleasure. You may still be finding that your intention is to please your partner with a certain behaviour but she does not always notice.

You can increase your mutual good feelings by communicating to your partner your desire to please her. Do not always rely on her being aware enough to notice everything you do for her. You will both be able to give pleasure with more enjoyment if at times you are able to communicate your desire to please, as well as your awareness that your partner has done something to give you pleasure.

Go back to your diary and begin recording what you did to please your partner. You should now have a better idea of what pleases him, after going through the previous exercises.

As before, choose a quiet time at the end of the week to sit down and swap your diaries. Practise communicating your desire to please your partner. 'I washed the dishes because I thought you looked tired.' 'I gave you a kiss because I wanted to feel close to you.'

When your partner tells you what she did, respond positively. For example, 'Thanks for doing those dishes, it was a great help'.

Now try to communicate to your partner, at least once a day, what you did to please him, as well as remembering to tell your partner when he does something you find pleasing.

Step 5 Are there any changes you need to make to pleasure giving? For example, in your relationship your partner may tell you about once a week that you look nice. You could request her to double the number of times she mentions how nice you look.

Do not expect your partner, at the moment, to do anything for you that he finds objectionable. You will need communication and problem-solving skills to resolve this problem. We'll describe those later.

Are there any more ways of giving pleasure that you can introduce? Is there any major area in your relationship from the list in Step 1 where there is little or no pleasure giving? Ask your partner what she would like, or make a list of what you would like. Then discuss the list with your partner. Is he willing to try this new way of giving you pleasure?

Try to increase the range of pleasure giving activities. If you only do one thing to please your partner per day, try to increase this to two or three per day. Use your communication skills to let your partner know that you have tried to please her.

Step 6 This is about asking for affection and pleasure giving. Many people in relationships fall into the trap of expecting their partner to know when they would like affection or pleasure giving. Your own experience should help you realise that your partner does not always know what you would like. It is therefore important, if you are to find the relationship as satisfactory as possible, that you be prepared to ask for what you would like.

As with all other behaviour, affection does not happen 'naturally'. You learn to respond to someone else affectionately. In a successful long-term relationship you need to learn when each of you wants affection or pleasure giving.

All of us are different, and we feel differently, at different times. So it is unreasonable to expect that anyone automatically would know how we are feeling and what we would like. The best chance to get what you would like is to ask.

We believe that it is better to ask for affection and pleasure giving than to feel upset or resentful when you do not get them. Of course, it is good to receive affection or pleasure giving unexpectedly, but it is important to develop skills of being able to ask for affection or pleasure giving.

Sit down together, in a place where you will not be interrupted and practise asking for pleasure giving.

For example:

'I feel sad and would like you to comfort me with a hug.'

'I am really tired. It would be very nice if you would tidy up for me.'

'I am really happy. I would like you to kiss me.'

At first, as with the other exercises, you may feel uncomfortable and awkward, but with practice you will find this easier. No-one ever died of awkwardness.

Now, along with asking your partner to recognise when you are doing something to give him pleasure, you should practise asking for pleasure giving or affection from your partner in your day-to-day life. Begin by asking her to do one thing to give you pleasure each day, and then increase this to three or four things, including acts of affection, per day.

Step 7 As with earlier exercises, if you are having difficulties:

1 Check your self-talk.
2 Check that you have correctly followed the programme.
3 Use your communication skills.

Remember that the more pleasure you are prepared to give, the more you are likely to receive, and the more rewarding your relationship will become.

Beware of giving pleasure and immediately expecting something in return. It has been shown that couples who give pleasure to each other without expecting any immediate payback have more successful relationships than couples who expect an immediate return from their partners. In other words, you need to give pleasure to your partner as a sign of your 'good faith' in the relationship. Your partner should eventually respond to your demonstration of affection and commitment, and that's more valuable than an immediate payback.

Be careful that you do not slip back into your old habits. Make sure that you keep up your new pleasing behaviour. The more you practise any part of this programme, the easier you will find the changes, and the longer you practise, the more your new behaviour will become a habit.

If you find yourself returning to your old habits, pick up the programme and start again. You will probably be able to go through the steps faster, a second time around.

Some more coupling suggestions

1 The 'Cookie Jar' or 'Biscuit Barrel'

Most couples find this exercise fun. Get two jars and put your name on one and your partner's name on the other. Each of you then writes on slips of paper the 'gifts' you would like to receive from the other person. As with your coupling ideas, the gifts should vary in 'size', e.g. from 'a hug' to 'a night out' to 'a holiday at the beach'. Your 'cookies' can be objects, e.g. a record, a bottle of perfume, or activities e.g. a foot rub, a massage.

Whenever you feel like doing something nice for your partner, go to her cookie jar, take out a request, and deliver her 'cookie'. When you have delivered the requested 'cookie', to your partner's appreciation, we hope, you can return the request to her cookie jar for a future repeat, if that's appropriate.

The cookie jar technique comes from the observation that in long-standing relationships the partners would often like to do nice things for each other, but are stuck for ideas. You may notice this yourself, twice a year, on birthdays and Christmas.

The advantages of the cookie jar technique are that it gives you information – you know what your partner would like to receive from you – but it retains spontaneity – it's entirely up to you as to when you feel like dipping into your partner's cookie jar.

Many couples enjoy their cookie jars so much that they keep them going long after therapy is over. In families, the kids will often notice how much fun their parents are getting from their cookie jars, and ask for their own! That's fine; extending the cookie jar technique to the whole family will just build good feelings in the whole family.

You can update your cookie jar from time to time, by adding new requests or dropping out old ones. Do vary the cost of your cookies, so that there are always some your partner can give you without great expense or time.

Two points of caution about the cookie jar technique: it is not a way to make your partner do something he doesn't want to. So, if you pull out a slip with a request that is unacceptable to you, discard it and pull out another one. If you want your partner to change some part of his behaviour, that is dealt with in Chapters 6 and 7.

And second, don't punish your partner for trying to do something nice for you. If your partner comes over to deliver a 'cookie', such as a back-rub, and you're not in the mood, or you don't have time just then, don't react negatively. Reward her – 'It's nice of you to offer' – decline graciously – 'but I'm not in the mood right now' – and preferably make an alternative time to accept your cookie – 'How about after dinner?'

2 Special times

Some coupling is brief, a foot-rub, a hug, or a nice kiss. A special time is when you have set aside a substantial amount of time, like an afternoon or an evening, to do something special together, like going out to the movies or staying home to play cards. Our rule of thumb is that you should aim to have at least one special time a week.

We suggest that you take it in turns to arrange special times. This means that one of you takes full responsibility for making all of the arrangements for this special time, like booking tickets, or getting a baby-sitter, or preparing a special dinner. Next time, it's the other partner's turn.

Of course, you would look at your coupling menu, or discuss which movies are on at the moment, to make sure that what was planned will be enjoyable for both partners. But one partner does all of the arranging. The other one just keeps the time free.

In this way, special times become more gifts that you exchange with each other, in your relationship. This week one of you gives the other a fun night at the movies. Next week the second partner gives the first a special dinner at home, with candlelight and music.

Often, not knowing exactly where you're going or what you're doing adds freshness and excitement to the relationship, feelings that were probably there at the beginning, but sadly often fade. It's usually a good idea to tell each other what's appropriate to wear – shorts, dinner suit or wet suit? – but a bit of mystery can be fun.

3 Pleasure days

A pleasure day is a day, or at least part of a day, in which one of you tries to do as many pleasing things for the other as possible. Your diaries of pleasure giving can be good sources of ideas. Next time around, you swap over and the giver becomes the receiver. Doing pleasing things for your partner is a tangible expression of your love, and pleasure days can help to build that feeling.

Not surprisingly, pleasure days go together very well with sexual enhancement, although they are not meant to be only sexual. For the moment, try some non-sexual ways of giving pleasure. When you do Chapter 4, you can have some sexual pleasure days, as well.

'But it's so artificial'

We will keep dealing with this common objection to relationship improvement exercises, because many people express it. Yes, you're quite right. It is artificial, even the planned spontaneity. So are all learning programmes.

This manual sets out a structured learning programme, through which we hope you will acquire or strengthen good relationship skills. It does this largely by getting you to practise the skills as they are introduced. This is, of course, an artificial process.

It is sad that at the moment our society doesn't offer a more 'natural' (meaning less structured) opportunity for learning human relations skills and knowledge. Until it does, most of us will need more structured, catch-up programmes, like this one.

When you have mastered the various relationship skills, through learning, however artificial, and practice, however awkward, then you can use them 'naturally' and spontaneously in your improved relationship. For now, don't expect to run before you can toddle.

Establishing long-term plans for and souvenirs of your relationship

Any two people who have lived in a relationship together for some length of time share events and activities that become important for the relationship. These are souvenirs of mutual love, affection, romance and warmth in your relationship together.

For example, a particular holiday you spent together may become a souvenir; an activity that you always do with your partner may become a souvenir; a private joke about each other may become a souvenir. As well, there are the conventional souvenirs, such as the wedding rings, the home you live in, memories and photographs of your wedding, the birth of your children, significant stages of your children's development, and so on.

When a relationship becomes distressed, the couple may forget about the importance of the past good times that they had together. Their relationship becomes overrun with negative memories. The point of this exercise is to get you and your partner to share once again the good memories that bring you close together.

PRACTICAL EXERCISE
What souvenirs of your relationship do you have?

Make a time to sit down together and discuss your souvenirs. Here are some examples:

One couple had developed a response to ending arguments and that was for one of them to wave a card that had the word 'stop' on it. This always produced a stream of good feelings in both of them and usually ended the argument.

Another couple placed importance on the home that they had built themselves. With photographs of every stage, it represented the sharing and hard work in their relationship.

Breakfast in bed on Sunday morning was something another

couple ritually engaged in, and this produced a warm close feeling for both of them.

Recalling the hard times earlier in their relationship brought another couple closer together.

If you cannot think of any souvenirs of your relationship, start developing some now. Souvenirs can be objects, places, times or rituals that you both share and enjoy. Remember, even past bad events can become souvenirs that you can laugh about together.

While souvenirs of your relationship tend to emphasise the good past or present events, it is also important for partners in a long-term relationship to develop plans for the future together. It is a sign of trust that, together as a couple, you discuss and make plans for your future. You are saying to each other, by your actions, that the relationship is important to you and you want to plan for the future with each other.

A number of distressed couples we have seen have stopped making future plans. This leads to even more distress, because it appears as though they have given up on the relationship. There is no point waiting until 'things are better' before you make future plans. Just the fact that you are prepared to make plans together will give you incentive to change now.

The plans couples make include building a home together, planning to have children, planning to go overseas or on holidays, planning to live in a certain area, or even planning social activities.

PRACTICAL EXERCISE
Make some plans for the future

Sit down together and talk over some of the plans you have for the future. Even just talking about future plans, whether they happen or not, can help you both feel more committed to the relationship.

Overall, the good things of the past, as well as the hoped for good events in the future, are all important in adding to the feelings of enjoyment and sense of commitment that you both have for your relationship.

Some tips to help you get the most out of coupling

Tip 1 Communicate.
Whenever you engage in coupling, be sure to communicate your enjoyment to each other. The only way your partner is

definitely going to know you are enjoying yourself is if you tell
him. Do not leave it up to your partner to try and guess
whether you are enjoying yourself. It is a mistake to assume
that your partner will know that you are enjoying yourself.
Even if there are other signs that you are having a good time,
still tell your partner. It is nice to hear from someone that she
is enjoying herself. This will add to enjoyment for both of
you.

Practise before you go out together what you could say to
your partner to indicate your enjoyment. For example:

'I am having a great time, darling. Let's do this again soon.'

'This is fabulous. I had forgotten what great fun this could
be.'

Do not give compliments or pleasant statements barbed with
criticism. For example:

'This is good, but why didn't you think to do this years ago?'

'I like you doing that, but why don't you do it more often?'

Statements, like the last two, differ from the first two,
because there is an implied criticism of the other person. It is
possible to suggest that you are having a great time and would
like to repeat what you are doing without criticising your
partner. Criticism will only make your partner angry or upset
and you will spoil your nice time together.

Planning ahead, so that you know what you will say, will
help prevent you from slipping into statements that imply
criticism. If you are not used to making nice statements to
each other, this will not happen spontaneously. So plan,
ahead of time, what compliments you could make to your
partner, and how you will express your pleasure.

At the same time, you may like to think ahead how you will
respond to a pleasant or complimentary statement made by
your partner. For example:

'That was really nice of you to say that.'

'I am really glad that you told me how much you are enjoying
yourself.'

During your coupling, try to be sensitive to the good things
that are happening, and become more insensitive to

unpleasant moments. You will both have a history of unpleasant interactions together, and this may slip out during your coupling. This is only to be expected as your old habits will not change overnight. Unless it is a very important issue to you, plan to become less sensitive to statements or behaviour you dislike in your partner and try to focus on what you like. Then comment to your partner on the nice things he is doing. The more you notice good things, the more enjoyable your time together will be.

Unless it is genuinely urgent, do **not** use your coupling time to discuss problems. Reserve it for making and sharing good feelings. Plan other times to discuss problems (see Chapter 6).

Tip 2 Watch your self-talk or what you say to yourself.
How you feel about things is largely determined by how you think about them, so what you think to yourself has a very important bearing on how much you will enjoy yourself in your relationship. It will either enhance your ability to act positively in your relationship, or it may prevent you from improving your relationship. (For further discussion refer to the section in Chapter 5 'feeling better by thinking straighter'.)

We have mentioned the importance of self-talk a number of times in this chapter. It is particularly important if you are having any difficulties carrying out any of the previous suggestions.

We believe, as we said earlier, that what you say to yourself influences how you feel, and so what you do. For example:

When your partner does something that pleases you:

Unhelpful self-talk:	'What is she up to? What does she want from me?'
Feeling:	Mistrust
Behaviour:	Ignore your partner, or say 'What are you up to?'
Result:	Unpleasant interaction between you. Partner disappointed.

Instead you could try saying to yourself:

Helpful self-talk:	'That is really nice of her to do that. I will say so.'
Feeling:	Pleasure

Behaviour:	Kiss partner and say, 'Thank you for doing that.'
Result:	Enjoyable interaction between you.

Look at this situation: You and your partner have been enjoying yourselves at dinner when he makes a slightly negative comment:

Unhelpful self-talk:	'There he goes again, always criticising.'
Feeling:	Anger
Behaviour:	Retort, 'Why are you so critical?'
Result:	Argument.

Instead you could try:

Helpful self-talk:	'I found that comment hurtful, but I can cope with feeling hurt. Is it worth saying anything? We have had such a nice time.'
Feeling:	Hurt
Behaviour:	Say, 'I have been really enjoying our time together but I found that last statement hurtful. Is there anything wrong?'
Result:	A brief discussion that sorts out the difficulty. Then the couple continue to enjoy themselves.

When you do something nice for your partner, and she doesn't respond:

Unhelpful self-talk:	'The ungrateful so-and-so. She hasn't even noticed that I did that for her.'
Feeling:	Anger
Behaviour:	Acting out anger by slamming the door
Result:	Your partner responds angrily to your anger, and you have a fight.

Instead:

Helpful self-talk:	'That's disappointing, but I can't expect her to notice every time I try to please. I'll share it anyway.'
Feeling:	Disappointed
Behaviour:	Say, 'I felt disappointed when you didn't notice my trying to be nice.'
Result:	Your partner realises you are trying to be nice, and responds in the same way.

As a final example, you and your partner are having difficulty finding a time when you could couple together:

Unhelpful self-talk:	'There is no way I am giving up anything to go out with him.'
Feeling:	Anger and resentment
Behaviour:	Say angrily, 'There is no way I am giving up my time.'
Result:	A stand-off: no-one gets what they want. Both feel bad.
Helpful self-talk:	'I will feel disappointed missing out on my hobby but I can cope with that. If our relationship is to improve, both of us will need to give up some individual activities.'
Feeling:	Disappointed, but willing to try
Behaviour:	Say, 'I could miss my hobby and we could go out that night. Our relationship is important to me.
Result:	Partner is very loving and suggests a permanent arrangement that is more suitable to both. Both feel good.

Changing your self-talk will not be easy. The first step is to discover when, with whom and under what circumstances your self-talk is unhelpful. The best way to do this is to take note of what you are thinking to yourself when you get angry or upset. These feelings are often a sign that your self-talk is unhelpful. Then, using the examples as guides, write out, on small cards, more helpful self-talk.

Practise saying this more helpful self-talk to yourself. Take your cards out and read them, even if you are not in the situation that caused the problems.

When you know that you are going to face a situation that has caused you problems, rehearse how you are going to think. Carry your new, helpful self-talk with you, and read the card before you go into the situation, or read it again in the middle of the situation.

Example
Joan knew that she always had unhelpful self-talk when she went to please her husband Arthur.

Joan's unhelpful self-talk: 'I am always pleasing him; he never does anything for me.'

Joan recognised the destructiveness of such a self-statement. It made her angry and less likely to do anything nice for Arthur. Joan carefully looked at what she was saying to herself and wrote on a small card some new self-talk.

Joan's helpful self-talk: 'Even though in the past neither of us did pleasing things for each other, it does not mean that we cannot change now. I feel it is important to our relationship that I give Arthur pleasure even though he may not immediately return it.'

Joan read this card carefully to herself every time she did something pleasing for Arthur. After some practice, she was able to say this to herself as automatically as she had been able to say the unhelpful self-talk.

Your view of your relationship, and so your feelings and actions, can change dramatically, depending on how you look at it. This means, however, being prepared to give up your old ways of thinking and that will take time and effort.

Only you can know what your self-talk is, and only you can take the responsibility for changing it, as your individual contribution to improving the relationship. Don't be disheartened if you haven't entirely caught on to the idea of self-talk yet. It takes time to learn to recognise when your self-talk is unhelpful, time to practise more helpful self-talk, and time before that more helpful self-talk becomes a habit. We believe that the tenor of your self-talk is very important to your relationship and we will keep mentioning self-talk thoughout the book. If you are finding it difficult to alter your self-talk, you may find it easier at first to look for an example that is similar to your situation and to practise the 'helpful self-talk' this way.

Do you need to go back and revise the relationship myths to help you change your self-talk?

3
Communicating better

'He just doesn't understand how I feel.'
'She can't see why it's important to me!'
'He wouldn't know how I feel, and even if he did, he wouldn't care.'
'I can't understand why she does the things she does.'

Sometimes it's obvious that communication in a relationship is missing or poor. Neither partner in the above example really knows or accepts how the other feels. Both feel misunderstood and ignored by each other. What communication does occur becomes increasingly coercive, with each partner trying to nag the other into agreeing with him or her. Or it just all gets so unpleasant, they give up trying and hardly talk to each other at all.

Sometimes a couple will tell us that they have good communication. 'We talk about everything all the time.' And yet they have lots of fights, or still feel that their relationship is unsatisfactory.

Of course, some couples do communicate well. Good luck to them, they won't gain much from this chapter. But sometimes this 'good communication' is an illusion, consisting of lots of chatter about unimportant issues, while carefully avoiding the hot ones. Or they do both air their opinions on the problems in the relationship, but both do so at the same time, talking over each other, primarily listening each to him or herself.

Typically this cross-complaining escalates into another fight. Fights hurt, so after a while they stop trying to communicate because 'It's useless trying to talk to him'.

Good communication is essential for a successful relationship. Communication is the basic process through which you share feelings and information, reach an understanding of each other, and solve the problems facing the relationship. It is literally the glue that holds the relationship together. Without it, a relationship will inevitably fall apart.

Given how important communication is in human relationships, it's a tragedy that no-one teaches us about it properly. Such a complex behaviour doesn't come 'naturally', any more than driving a car or cooking a good chocolate cake or any other skill.

At school, we may learn how scientists or historians or whoever communicate through formal written statements. In the home, we may learn how our parents communicate, but unfortunately that wasn't always the greatest example. In business, we may learn to communicate through memos, or orders, or accounts. From novels and movies and television we can get some very strange ideas about how people communicate.

No-one sits down and says, 'Here is how adults living together in a love relationship communicate with each other effectively, so that they both feel understood and accepted by each other, and neither of them feels he or she has to bottle up or deny important feelings.'

Well, this chapter does. Nearly all couples we have seen, in or out of therapy, would benefit from carefully working through the information and exercises in this chapter. It often isn't as easy as it first looks. Couples trying to improve their communication go through several typical stages.

At first, they are usually aware that things aren't right; they may correctly identify part of the problem as poor or missing communication, or they may make complaints like those in the examples above. Either way, although they realise something is wrong, they don't know what to do about it. This usually results in confusion or frustration.

Then, through therapy or reading something like this chapter, they become aware of what is needed for good communication, and how to do it. This usually results in feelings of awkwardness and embarrassment. Initially, it can be hard to follow all the steps correctly. Strong feelings may be aroused as they begin to communicate about previously avoided issues. It often feels silly to have to follow instructions from a book on how to talk to each other.

But then two things happen. First, they find that good communication skills work. They may quickly feel better about each other and more optimistic about the relationship. Even a difficult session, practising communication about a very hurtful problem, can at least show that you are beginning to tackle the obstacles in front of your relationship.

And second, with repeated practice, good communication becomes easier, and eventually a natural part of their relationship. It becomes as automatic to communicate well, as it had been to communicate badly, or not even try.

You will probably go through the same stages, with much the same feelings. That's OK. It just means you react like most people. However difficult or discouraging it may feel at times, especially when you are just starting, persistence will pay off. You must communicate well to have a good relationship. So read and discuss this chapter, and then set yourselves some times to start the exercises.

THE BASIC INGREDIENTS OF COMMUNICATION

There are three basic elements in the communication process. You need all three, working properly, for good communication. They are:

1 Sending information to your partner. This may be information about your feelings or thoughts, or factual information about something to do with the relationship, or an answer to a message from your partner. It is usually accompanied or may even be totally transmitted by non-verbal messages from you. In clear communication, your verbal and non-verbal messages are saying much the same things.

2 Receiving information from your partner. This involves actually hearing what your partner has to say, but also seeing or feeling your partner's non-verbal messages. It can be confusing and frustrating when your partner's verbal and non-verbal messages don't seem to match.

3 Processing the information from your partner. This involves thinking about what your partner said or did, and what it means. It's at this stage that your self-talk about your partner, yourself and the relationship plays a key role in determining how you will finally respond.

To get all three ingredients of communication going successfully, you will need three skills, and helpful self-talk. We will now describe each of these four behaviours, so that you can begin to use them.

Levelling

Levelling means telling your partner, clearly and reasonably calmly, how you feel. It means using 'I' messages, not 'You' messages.

You messages:

'You make me angry.'
'You just ignore me, you never pay me any attention.'
'You never help me.'
'Only you can make me happy.'

I messages:

'I feel angry when you get home from work and just sit in front of the TV.'
'I feel upset when we do not talk to each other.'
'I feel angry when you sit down while I am working.'
'I feel happy when I am with you.'

Levelling is the opposite of hiding your feelings. It saves your partner from having to mind-read your feelings, which is important. As we discussed in Chapter 1, mind-reading is often wrong, particularly when the relationship is distressed, and it can make things unnecessarily worse. Telling your partner exactly how you are feeling saves her from trying to mind-read you.

You may also have noticed that one of our examples above was levelling about good feelings. This is very important. If the only time you level is when you feel bad, you will wind up with the impression that the only feelings in your relationship are bad ones. If that were true, you'd be silly to stay in it!

In Chapter 2 we talked about how to make your relationship more rewarding and enjoyable. Basically, we think people should stay in relationships only because they find them good, not out of a misguided sense of obligation or a desire to be a martyr.

A crucial step in making your relationship rewarding is to share your good feelings. A basic law of human behaviour is that people are more likely to do things which make them feel good. If your partner does something that makes you feel good, and you would like him to do it more often, reward it! Tell your partner how she made you feel good.

> 'I like it when you help me.'
> 'I feel pleased when you have cooked dinner.'
> 'I like it when you look nice.'
> 'I think it is really nice when you think of me and ring me during the day.'
> 'I enjoy your company when we go out to dinner.'
> 'I find it very helpful when you get the kids off to school.'

Most of us have some difficulty with compliments, both giving them and receiving them. We have been influenced by the British stiff upper lip tradition that praising people too much gives them swelled heads. Besides, people ought to do 'the right thing' just because it's right, shouldn't they?

Hogwash! How are they, including your partner, to know that they have done the right thing unless you tell them? We are not suggesting you go overboard and smother each other with compliments. We are pointing out the laws of human nature – people are much more influenced by rewards than punishment – and we suggest you make sensible use of it in your relationship. Share good feelings, and they will multiply.

Levelling with 'I' messages also shows that you are accepting responsibility for your own feelings, and not trying to put that responsibility onto your partner. 'You' messages are often blaming exercises. Even if the 'you' messages are compliments, you are giving all the responsibility for your wellbeing to your partner, and that is impossible.

'You make me feel hurt.'
'You make me feel happy.'
'You upset me when you do that.'
'You make me feel good.'

Obviously it is true that your partner's actions can **influence** how you feel. But it is not true that your partner's actions **determine** how you feel. How you feel about anything is finally determined by how you think about it, which is **your** responsibility. Later, we'll go into detail about how your self-talk influences communication, and what to do about it.

For now, let's focus on the situation where your partner has done something that has led to your feeling bad. In this case, you should level with what we call an X-Y-Z statement. This is a statement which has the following form:

'When you do X in situation Y, I feel Z.'

For example:

'When you come home late, without telling me before, I feel angry.'
'When you criticise me, when we are with friends, I feel hurt.'
'When you nag me, to do the household jobs, I feel annoyed.'
'When you do not make nice statements about my appearance, when we go out, I feel let down.'
'When you do not comment, when I give you a surprise gift, I feel hurt.'
'When you do not help me, with household tasks, I feel unhappy.'

Notice how precise this kind of levelling statement is. You are telling your partner exactly what he does, under exactly what circumstances, and exactly how you feel about it. This is important.

Typically when couples argue, there are several patterns in their communication. They character-assassinate each other: each blames the problems in the relationship on the faulty character of the other, e.g. 'If you weren't so lazy' and 'You ought to be more considerate.'

They kitchen-sink: they drag everything into the discussion

but the kitchen sink. And they sidetrack: they may start talking about one issue, but they quickly go off down a number of sidetracks, so that nothing ever gets resolved.

'Why can't we go out more often.'

'How can we afford to, while you waste so much money!'

'Well, I wouldn't have to rush the shopping so much if you helped me instead of always going to the races.'

'There you go again, nagging me about my one leisure activity. You're just like your mother was.'

'You always blame everything on my mother. What sort of an example was your father?'

'At least he's never tried to interfere like your family does.'

'You're just plain selfish, like your father was. If you think I'm going to be treated like your mother was, you've got another think coming!'

'Your sister can keep her stickybeak out of our affairs, too!'

'At least I can talk to her. You're never here when I need you.'

'That's typical of you, changing the subject when you're losing the argument.'

and so on.

Notice how both people in the conversation above are making sweeping generalisations about each other. The original topic has long been lost; the name of the game now is tit-for-tat.

The only true generalisation in relationships is that generalisations in relationships are rarely true. It may be true that your partner often does something you don't like, or rarely does something you would like, but it is unlikely to be true that she 'always' or 'never' does it.

Accusing your partner through a generalisation distracts you both from what really happened on this occasion, and usually draws a defensive response from him, because he knows what you are accusing him of isn't 'always' true. His defensiveness will encourage more kitchen-sinking and sidetracking, leading you both to conclude how dreadful your partner is.

If it really were true that you had married a person with deficient character – low, mean, scheming, untrustworthy, inconsiderate, selfish, dull and boring – the more fool you in the first place, and how silly you must be to stay in the relationship in the second place.

Criticism aimed at your partner's 'character' or 'personality' we call destructive feedback. Apart from sticking a negative label on your partner, it doesn't go anywhere. It usually just gets a hostile reaction back.

Constructive feedback, in contrast, is criticism aimed at your partner's behaviour. It is constructive, because she can then change her behaviour, if she wants to. This is exactly what an X-Y-Z levelling statement does: it gives your partner information on how you feel about a particular piece of her behaviour. She can then change it.

PRACTICAL EXERCISE

Levelling

1 Put aside about ten minutes each day to practise levelling on good and bad feelings. Do not spend any more than ten minutes. Do not get into arguments (see Chapter 5).

2 Each of you think of something the other has done that led to your feeling good. (Yes, good. It's just as important to level on good feelings as bad.) When you have an action of your partner's in mind, make up an X-Y-Z levelling statement about it, and say it to him or her.

For example: 'When you helped me clear up last night, even though it was my turn, I felt good.'

The partner receiving the levelling statement need not respond at all, just listen.

If you are out of practice at saying good things to each other, this exercise may be surprisingly difficult. You may feel awkward and embarrassed, and have trouble keeping eye contact. That's OK: no-one ever died of awkwardness. It just shows you how much out of practice you are, so all the more reason to try.

When you feel more comfortable, and are able to put together an X-Y-Z levelling statement, you can practise levelling in your day-to-day interactions. In the future, look for appropriate chances to level on good feelings.

3 Now, in the same session, each of you think of something the other did recently that led to your feeling bad. When you have it

in mind, make up an X-Y-Z statement about it. Be as precise as you can, and keep it brief.

For example: 'When you were sarcastic towards me in front of our friends, I felt humiliated.'

At this stage, the partner receiving the levelling message should **not** reply, just listen (more about this in a minute).

Be careful to level about a single incident. Even if it's something your partner has done before, or something you think he or she does often, focus on one recent example. He or she will get the message just as clearly, and you avoid the risk of over-generalising.

The X and Y of a levelling statement should be actions and situations that anyone present could have seen, not interpretations or assumptions that only occur in your mind.

For example:

not 'When you tried to make a fool out of me in front of our friends . . .'
'When you tried to upset me . . .'
'When you accused me . . .'
'When you blamed me . . .'
'When you tried to hurt me . . .'

but 'When you said I was incompetent in front of our friends . . .'
'When you said that you didn't like what I was wearing . . .'
'When you sounded angry when you were asking about the cheque book . . .'
'When you looked upset when you spoke about the children . . .'
'When you did not speak to me, when I said ''Hello'' . . .'

The Z only you can supply, since you are the only person who really knows how you feel, but do make sure it is a feeling, not a thought.

For example:

not 'I felt that you were having a go at me.'
but 'I felt angry.'

Some people, particularly men, have trouble reporting feelings. Make sure your Z is an emotion. If you follow 'I feel' with 'that' or 'as if', you are probably going to state a thought not a feeling. Feelings can usually be described with one word: you do not need to make a statement.

For example: happy, glad, pleased, important, sexy, joyful, great, good.
unhappy, angry, sad, upset, hurt, annoyed, disappointed, frustrated.

Practise making levelling statements until you are sure you can make them, briefly and precisely.

Listening

At first glance you might think this is easy; just point an ear in the right direction and you ought automatically to be listening. Unfortunately, it isn't always that easy.

Time and time again in marital therapy we have seen two reasonably intelligent people, neither of them with any hearing problems, seated only a small distance apart, both completely unable to repeat back a simple levelling statement that the other has just made.

Each is busy listening all right, but to himself or herself! Each one assumes that he knows what the other is going to say – they mind-read each other – so there is no need actually to listen to the other person. Instead, each is busy writing the next salvo inside his head, checking the script for the next clever statement. When it's ready, he will ignore or interrupt what the other person really said, and issue his clever statement.

By listening, we mean actively following what your partner says, rather than guessing, mind-reading or interrupting. It can be difficult not to interrupt when your partner says something that you disagree with, but if you start to talk over each other, communication will usually break down into an argument or silence.

There is a neat trick to help you listen actively: pretend to be a tape recorder. Whenever you should be listening to your partner, especially if he is trying to level to you about his feelings, set yourself the goal of being able to repeat back to him what he just said to you.

We are not suggesting that you will always need to repeat back to each other every statement made in the relationship. That would obviously be cumbersome and silly. We are suggesting that when you and your partner are trying to

communicate with each other on important issues, you should be able to repeat what your partner said to you.

To help you master this skill of active listening, we suggest that when you are practising communication skills, through the exercises in this chapter and at other times, you play back to your partner your mental 'tape recording' of what she just said to you.

Levelling: 'When you come home late, without telling me before, I feel angry.'

Listening: 'You said that when I come home late, without telling you before, you feel angry.'

You see, you can't repeat back what your partner said unless you have listened carefully. Of course, it is a clumsy way to have a conversation, and you wouldn't what to do it all the time. But as a temporary measure, to help you improve your listening skills, and at any time in the future when the conversation is getting heated, it's a useful step.

PRACTICAL EXERCISE

Levelling and Listening

Repeat the exercise of each of you levelling to the other about something your partner did that led to your feeling bad. This time, the person receiving the levelling statement should 'parrot' back what was said, as in the example above.

When you can parrot back levelling statements easily, try

repeating them in your own words, **but** be careful not to change the meaning. For example:

'When you made the decision to chop the tree down in the garden without consulting me, I felt angry.'

'You said that, when I made the decision to chop the tree down in the garden without consulting you, you felt angry.'

'When you let the children go to the movies alone, I felt annoyed.'

'You said that when I permitted the children to go to the pictures by themselves, you felt annoyed.'

'When you broke my best china plate, I felt upset.'

'You felt upset when I broke your best china plate.'

Let your partner be the judge of whether or not he thinks you have heard what he said. If this takes some discussion, that's fine; it means you are trying to understand each other.

'When you smashed our brand new car, I felt disappointed.'

'Me smashing our new car disappointed you, is that right?'

'Yes.'

You won't always hear your partner correctly the first time. That need not be a problem, nor lead to misunderstanding. It is up to your partner to tell you she doesn't think you heard her correctly. For example:

'When you did not remember my birthday this year, I felt let down.'

'I let you down by not remembering your birthday, is that right?'

'That wasn't quite what I meant. I meant that when you didn't remember my birthday this year, I felt let down, not that you have let me down.'

'So, when I didn't remember your birthday this year, you felt let down.'

If you are having trouble repeating what your partner has said in words that clearly express her meaning, go back and 'parrot' what she has said.

Validating

Validating is the key to achieving mutual understanding in a relationship. It can also be difficult to do. It means **accepting** what your partner says about his feelings, not denying his feelings, nor insisting that he should feel as you do or as you think he should feel. For example:

not 'It's silly for you to feel like that!'
not 'But I didn't mean to make you feel like that!'
but 'Yes, I can see that's how you feel.'

Validating does not necessarily mean that you **agree** with your partner; it does mean that you accept his point of view, even though it may be different from yours. This does not mean that you are 'giving in', only that you are respecting each other's rights to be individuals.

As we said in Chapter 1, it is not necessary that the two partners in a relationship think and feel the same about everything. It **is** necessary that they accept each other's right to think and feel differently, when that happens.

Levelling   'When you come home late, without telling me before, I feel angry.'
Listening   'You said that when I come home late, without telling you before, you feel angry. Is that right?'
Validating   'Yes, I can see how that would make you angry.'

Notice that validating means just **accepting** your partner's feelings; no excuses, no defensiveness, just acceptance. This can be hard to do at first, especially if your partner has levelled with you that she feels bad about something you did, when you didn't mean to make her feel bad.

Intent and effect

This last situation is where what you intend and its effect don't match. You will have experienced this many times: you say something to someone, intending to be friendly or helpful, and they take it completely differently, as though you were being rude or aggressive.

Under these circumstances, it's easy to be defensive and say something like: 'But you shouldn't feel like that; I didn't mean to make you feel that way.'

What you are really saying is that the other person doesn't have the right to his own feelings, but instead he should feel as you tell him to. In other words, you think you can control your partner's feelings. Which is silly.

When you realise that your partner is levelling about bad feelings that come from a mismatch between what you intend and its effect, it's important to validate her feelings, and not to deny them by becoming defensive. You can state what your intent really was, **but** be careful not to do this in a way which stops you from fully accepting your partner's feelings.

Validating when intent doesn't match effect	'Yes, I can see how my being late would make you angry. I didn't intend to make you angry, but I can see that that's the effect it would have on you.'

Sometimes people have difficulty validating their partners' feelings because they wouldn't feel as their partners do under those circumstances. She will say, 'But I can't validate that, because I don't really **understand** why he feels like that.'

Let us make it clear that validating does not necessarily mean that you understand **why** your partner feels as she does, only that you understand and accept **how** she feels. Sometimes you will fully understand each other's feelings, and that's fine. But sometimes you won't. You are two different people who will sometimes react differently, and you won't always understand why your partner feels as he does. That need not be a problem, so long as you accept how he feels.

PRACTICAL EXERCISE
Levelling, Listening and Validating

Now you should do some more communication practice, this time taking it in turns to level, while the other listens and validates.

When you are practising, it can be helpful to make a cassette recording of some of your practice sessions. After the practice, play back the tape, but with only one question in mind: 'How could I have done that better?' The purpose of this procedure is to help you check your own progress, not to check your partner's.

This is a further example of the general point we made in the Introduction. None of our advice or suggestions should become weapons for you to use in new arguments. 'You didn't level properly!' 'Well, you didn't validate me before!'

If you do that to these procedures, you will lose their possible benefit. We'll have more to say shortly about the best frame of mind for good communication, but looking for points to score over each other isn't it.

'BUT IT DOES MATTER THAT WE DISAGREE'

Yes, it can. That will depend on how often and over what issues. If you genuinely disagree with each other over a very large number of important issues in your relationship, and you are unable to resolve those differences to your mutual satisfaction using the techniques in Chapter 6, then you may have to face the fact that you are in the wrong relationship.

But not all differences matter that much. Sometimes you may exchange some levelling, listening and validating over an issue, and eventually recognise that you do feel differently about it but that this difference isn't really important.

You may simply conclude by saying to each other, 'I see that's how you feel about it. It isn't how I feel about it, but I accept that it's how you feel about it.'

For example, one of you may like red wine, the other likes white wine, and so what? Unless you are about to buy six dozen of only one kind or the other, this difference need not really trouble your relationship.

On the other hand, sometimes your differences do represent potential problems for your relationship because they are over major issues, like which school to send a child to, where to go for your holidays, how to manage the family finances, and so on. They can't just be shrugged off, because eventually you do need to reach agreement on what to do.

The communication skills described in this chapter are not meant to solve these problems. They are meant, as we said, to generate feelings of acceptance and understanding. In doing this, they will identify issues about which you feel differently, and some of those differences are problems for your relationship.

To solve those problems, by resolving the important differences between you, you will use the problem-solving skills in Chapter 6. For now, this means you will have to put those problems into the 'Waiting-to-be-solved' basket until you work your way to Chapter 6.

This can be frustrating – having identified some of the problems in your relationship, you will naturally want to solve them. But you can only master one set of relationship skills at a time, and we believe it is essential to share your feelings first, before you attempt to solve the underlying problems. If you don't, the feelings won't go away; they will only hamper your attempts at problem solving.

So get yourselves a piece of paper, give it a heading, 'Waiting-to-be-solved', and as you identify important differences and problems between you, record them to use in Chapter 6.

SELF-TALK FOR BETTER COMMUNICATION

What we say to ourselves influences how we feel and what we do. This is the principle underlying our discussions of the relationship myths: your attitudes and beliefs about love and relationships influence how you feel and what you do in your relationship.

The same is true of communication, and you will recall that several of the myths refer to communication. You might like to go back and refresh those in your mind.

Now we are going to look at how your immediate thoughts in the situation can influence your attempts to communicate better and how your self-talk about communication can be helpful or unhelfpul.

Below we have set out, for each of the three communication skills, examples of both unhelpful and helpful self-talk. Whenever you are having difficulty communicating, check your own self-talk! That will often be the cause of your difficulty, and the answer is to change what you are saying to yourself.

Only you can know what you think, and only you can change what you are thinking, so only you can take responsibility for checking and, when appropriate, changing your self-talk.

Helpful and unhelpful self-talk when you are communicating

1 When you are levelling

Unhelpful self-talk:
'There's no point telling her how I feel. She doesn't care.'

Helpful self-talk:
'I know I will feel uncomfortable or anxious when I level but I can cope with those feelings.'

'If I let him close to me again, I'll only be hurt again.'

'She ought to know how I feel. It's obvious. We've been through this before.'

'If our relationship is to be good, we must communicate, so now I'll try.'
'We may not have communicated well in the past, but that's no reason to assume we can't now.'

2 When you are listening
Unhelpful self-talk:
'What right has he to feel like that!'
'It's silly for her to feel like that!'
'I didn't mean it that way. I'm not going to let him get away with that!'

Helpful self-talk:
'It's my turn to listen now; I can always level later.'
'Now, listen! What is she saying?'
'I can put my point of view later. Listen now!'

3 When you are validating
Unhelpful self-talk:
'If I give in now he will have it all his way.'

'I can't agree with that; it's not how I feel.'

'I didn't mean it that way. It's silly for her to feel like that.'

Helpful self-talk:
'I can validate his point of view without surrendering mine.'
'We are two individuals who have the right to think and feel differently.'
'I don't have the right to tell other people how they ought to feel.'

If you need more help with changing your self-talk refer to the section on 'Feeling better by thinking straighter and acting constructively' in Chapter 5.

UNSPOKEN FEARS AND STAND-OFFS

When a relationship is distressed, it's common for both partners to get into 'you-ortas'. Each will say to the other: 'You ought to do this and that, and then everything would be fine.' To which the reply is, 'No, you ought to do that, and then everything would be fine.'

This is what we call a stand-off. Both partners are waiting for the other to make the first move. If you get stuck in this situation, you can stay there forever, or at least until one of you gets sick of it and quits the relationship.

Often the stand-off in a relationship is occurring because of an underlying problem which neither partner has openly discussed. These underlying problems usually fall into one of two categories.

1 One (or both) of the partners is frightened that the other partner doesn't really find her attractive and doesn't really want to stay in the relationship. Because of this fear, she will keep playing the 'prove-you-love-me' game. This consists of continually setting up situations in which he is supposed to 'prove' he loves her.

Of course, nothing he does will ever prove this to her satisfaction because the doubt really lies in her mind, not in his behaviour or feelings. In the meantime, she will not make a clear commitment to the relationship because she won't believe it is worthwhile. After all, 'He doesn't love me any more'.

In this frame of mind, she withdraws her support from the relationship, waiting for her partner to demonstrate that he finds her attractive. She will not do anything nice for her partner until he does something nice for her.

If this situation continues, he will notice her withdrawal, and her impossible standards for the relationship. Then he often responds by also withdrawing. Thus a stand-off is created and maintained.

Each is saying to the other, 'You must first prove you love me [or do something for the relationship], before I will.' We have discussed earlier how this kind of 'tit-for-tat' trading is a sign that the relationship is distressed.

2 The second common unspoken fear is the 'power struggle'. This time the fear is of losing power in the relationship to the other partner. This fear usually stems from a basic lack of self-confidence. Doubting his ability to stay in control of the situation, he believes he cannot afford to budge a fraction or he will lose the lot.

Power struggles can be subtle and disguised. A pattern we have often seen is the 'bully and victim' routine. One of the partners in the relationship is so aggressive, emotionally or physically, towards the other that you wonder why the second one puts up with it.

Which is exactly the question. Why does she put up with it? The answer often seems to be because it's the only way she feels she can retain control of him. Frustrate him ('How could I possibly say I love him when he's so cruel to me?') until he does his lolly and lashes out (again). Once he cools down, his guilt about his outburst will keep him in line again for a while.

We are not saying that the apparent victim in this situation isn't genuinely hurt by the apparent bully's outbursts. We are saying that generally both of them work to maintain this system of interactions because both are afraid of losing power to each other by trying to be more reasonable. So we are back at a stand-off: 'I won't change how I act or feel towards you until you change how you act and feel towards me'.

John Gottman, an American psychologist working in the field of marital therapy, has called these unspoken fears 'hidden agendas'. They are unstated expectations about each other and the relationship that each partner brings to every discussion on every issue, and which therefore colour everything that is said.

Because they are not stated openly, they are never resolved. Instead they prevent the satisfactory resolution of problems in the relationship. No matter what the couple tries to do they end up in a 'stand-off'. If a couple repeatedly find themselves arguing over the same issues, or lots of trivial issues, without ever getting anywhere, this probably means they are really fighting over one of these hidden agendas, although neither of them would say so.

SELF-TALK AND SELF-ESTEEM

We believe that these unspoken fears are the result of lacking both self-esteem (at least in the area of love relationships) and relationship skills (or the willingness to use them).

It is beyond the scope of this book to go into detail about how to improve your self-esteem, but this is sometimes a prerequisite for improving your relationship. See the section on self-esteem in the introduction. Before you can ever have a genuinely successful relationship with anyone else, you must first have a reasonably good one with yourself! If you don't, these unspoken fears of losing love or power will be a permanent obstacle within your relationship.

Some good self-help resources on how to improve your self-esteem are: *Like Yourself and Others Will Too* by Abraham Twerski (Prentice-Hall) and *Talk to Yourself* by Charles Zastrow (Prentice-Hall). If self-help doesn't help, or isn't for you, and you believe a lack of self-esteem is a major contributor to the problems in your relationship, see a properly trained clinical psychologist.

ENDING STAND-OFFS

The relationship skills you can use to end stand-offs consist of changing both self-talk and behaviour. A common warning sign that you are heading into another stand-off is the thought, 'Here we go again!' Another reliable indicator is when you notice that the issue you are arguing over is really, if you look at it honestly, trivial. If you see these or other signs of an imminent stand-off, try both channels for ending it.

First, say to yourself: 'What am I saying to myself that is making me feel so bad? What could I say to myself that will help me to act more constructively?' Look at pages 60–1 for some guidelines. Ask yourself whether you are genuinely concerned about the issue being discussed, or are you really trying to make your partner prove he loves you or give in?

Second, ask yourself: 'Which relationship skill can I use to break this stand-off? Should I level (especially about my real fears)? Should I listen to my partner and validate her feelings? Is the discussion so heated, I should initiate time-out from it (explained in Chapter 5)?'

When you have decided on an appropriate relationship skill, do it! If that's very difficult, ask yourself, 'What's my real goal in this situation – short-term revenge or face-saving, or making a successful, long-term relationship?'

A RULE OF THUMB

Keep this rule of thumb in mind whenever communication becomes difficult or breaks down: What am I saying to myself? Is my self-talk   – realistic?
                                        – reasonable?
                                        – goal-oriented?
By goal-oriented, we mean is your self-talk aimed at

helping you get what you have currently set as your goal, a better relationship? When your partner hurts you, there is a temptation to hurt back. Your self-talk becomes revenge-oriented. That may produce some short-term satisfaction, but it may cost you your long-term goal.

Rational self-talk often involves being able to assess what is more important to you in the long run versus the short run. There are many ways of reacting in relationships that produce some short-term satisfaction but in the long run they only lead to further distress. But if you are prepared to put up with the short-term frustration, hurt or disappointment, that can pay off in the long run.

Example

Michelle always felt frustrated and upset that Sam, her husband, spent so much time involved with outside activities and organisations. In the past the only way she coped with this was by nagging Sam, until they got into an argument and she was able to vent all her frustration and aggression. The end result of these arguments was that Sam stayed out more often because he found her nagging and the fights they had very unpleasant.

By resorting to nagging Michelle made it less likely that she would get what she really wanted from the situation.

To change the situation she took a long hard look at herself. She realised that she partly became frustrated and upset because she was using unhelpful self-talk: 'There he goes again. I'll get him. He never wants to stay home with me. He is always going out.'

She wrote out some more helpful self-talk for herself: 'I feel frustrated and upset when Sam spends so much time away from home, but I can cope with these feelings. Nagging or fighting only makes the situation worse. I'll level with Sam about how I feel about his going out so much.'

Michelle waited until she and Sam had a quiet moment together. That meant waiting until the end of the week but she was beginning to cope better with her own feelings anyway, by practising her more rational self-talk.

Sam was so surprised when Michelle made the quiet, calm levelling statement that he immediately responded by suggesting that they work the problem out.

Michelle's self-talk had become goal-oriented, not revenge-oriented, and it helped her to get what she really wanted.

SOME TIPS FOR BETTER COMMUNICATION

1 The time to level is whenever you have strong feelings. Don't bottle up feelings: they don't go away; don't assume that your partner knows how you feel: that's an invitation to mind-read. The situation may not always be one in which you can level straight away; if so, look for the first appropriate opportunity.

2 The time to listen is when your partner tries to level with you. If he or she is levelling about good feelings, just listen. You might like to agree, but don't throw away the opportunity by joking about it. Accept compliments non-defensively. If he is levelling about bad feelings, listen and validate. Don't interrupt or become defensive; you can always express your point of view next.

3 It's just as important to level about good feelings as bad feelings. If you only ever share bad feelings, you will create the impression that there are only bad feelings in your relationship. If that's true, perhaps you should do something about it. If it isn't true, don't create the illusion.

4 Watch how you begin a discussion. Are you being aggressive or defensive? Are you mind-reading?

For example: **not** 'Well I don't suppose you want to go to your mother's on Saturday.' (said sarcastically)

but 'How do you feel about going to mother's on Saturday?'

or 'What would you like to do on Saturday?'

In other words, ask your partner's opinion or wishes, rather than guessing and then overreacting to your own guess.

5 Show your partner that you are interested. As much as 93 per cent of your emotional impact on another person is conveyed by non-verbal cues; only 7 per cent is carried by what you say. The rest is carried by the tone and volume of your speech, and by your body-talk, how you sit and so on.

For example, in a comfortable conversation, people have eye contact around half the time. Less eye contact and they look as though they are avoiding each other, more eye contact and they can look very aggressive towards each other. If you are very out of practice at sharing feelings, you may find it embarrassing and awkward when you start. Well, that's OK – no one ever died of embarrassment! Pick the appropriate helpful self-talk, and build up your eye contact.

6 Start practising your communication skills by discussing less important issues, so that you can concentrate on mastering the skills without strong feelings getting in the way. But don't ignore the difficult issues – they won't go away – once you feel you are able to level, listen and validate reasonably well, do it on the hard issues.

Now set aside time to practise communicating, if you haven't already done so. Three or four weekly practices, each of ten minutes is better than an hour at the end of the week. And you can start to look for naturally occurring opportunities to use your communication skills in your relationship.

4

Improving your sexual relationship

Your sexual relationship is an important part of coupling. It's obviously one of the good things you can do together. It ought not to be the only good thing you do together regularly, as sometimes it unfortunately becomes. But a good sexual relationship can be a major contribution to the rewardingness of the whole relationship. If you do the same thing, with the same person, at the same time of day, in the same location, for several or more years, you ought to expect it to lose some of its impact.

In fact, as many people discover, it can be downright boring. Since sexual dissatisfaction is the most common reason given for Australian marriages failing, sexual boredom is more than just an idle problem. We should logically expect some boredom to creep into long-standing sexual relationships, unless you do something deliberate and constructive to prevent it.

That's what sexual enhancement is all about. This chapter is for couples who don't regard themselves as having any particular sexual difficulty, but who do think their sexual relationship could use a boost.

That's an important distinction. If you think you have a sex problem, like premature ejaculation or missed orgasm, this programme won't be enough to solve it, even though it may be part of solving your problem. Self-help programmes for the common sex problems are set out clearly in *Treat Yourself to a Better Sex Life* by Harvey Gochros and Joel Fisher (Prentice-Hall).

If you want to try self-help for a sex problem, follow the

Inside Woody Allen

relevant programme in that book as closely as possible. Self-help failures often come from people not following their programmes. If self-help doesn't work or doesn't suit, see a clinically trained psychologist or other qualified therapist.

For the non-problematic couple, there is a very good sexual enhancement programme called **sensate focus**. The name is intended to emphasise the fact that the programme teaches people to focus on the pleasant and exciting sensations that come from a good sexual relationship.

It is a behavioural programme involving practical pleasuring exercises. As such, we think you enhance its effectiveness if you also get your heads into sexual gear. All the practical exercises in the world won't overcome the handicap of unrealistic sexual thoughts, attitudes and expectations. Sexually successful people, those who say they are sexually satisfied most of the time and who don't feel they have any real sexual problems, tend to use one or the other of two mental strategies during sex. They either focus on the pleasant feelings of sexual arousal and contact, or they increase their sexual response by imagining erotic fantasies.

People focussing on pleasant feelings are inclined to say that there isn't much at all going on in their minds, neither self-talk nor fantasies. Indeed, they find attempts to think or fantasise are distracting and interfere with sexual enjoyment. During sex, their mental content is an almost exclusive awareness of physical sensations and movement.

This is probably the more successful mental strategy for sexual satisfaction. It depends on two foundations. The person must be reasonably comfortable with her or his own sexuality, and reasonably confident and comfortable within the present relationship. Then you feel secure enough to stop worrying about your partner's reactions and instead can concentrate on your own.

The second successful strategy is the private blue movies scheme, imagining erotic fantasies. Typically, these involve the person in some sexual behaviour or relationship other than what is actually happening. Erotic fantasies like these seem to allow the person to gain, however imaginatively, arousal from sexual stimuli which are otherwise just unavailable. The arousal from these imagined stimuli adds to that coming from the actual sexual encounter, so that the daydreamer experiences higher levels of excitement.

There are three things to be said about this second technique for becoming sexually aroused.

1 There is nothing wrong with sexual fantasies. There is a world of difference between what you fantasise about and what you actually do. It isn't cheating on your partner to have sexual fantasies. If having erotic fantasies makes you a more rewarding sexual person to be with, that is hardly cheating.
2 One reservation about sexual fantasies: change them from time to time. If you consistently have the same sexual fantasy paired with sexual arousal, two unfortunate things can

happen. You can become dependent on that fantasy for arousal and unable to get aroused without it. And you will gradually find the content of your fantasy – the sexual act, or imagined partner – more and more arousing.

3 If you have to use it all the time, we wonder if there isn't something going wrong in the relationship because you don't find your partner sufficiently rewarding?

As well as having mental approaches that are successful in a sexual situation, you also need to have realistic expectations and attitudes about sex.

In Chapter 1 we discussed the popular myths about love and relationships that set people up for relationship difficulty and dissatisfaction.

Again, don't ask yourself whether or not you have believed these popular myths. When we asked people, by questionnaire, to indicate how strongly they held each of eight popular beliefs about sex, by and large no-one said they believed them all.

But when we asked people to describe their typical sexual behaviour, it became clear that most of them behaved as though they believed these popular beliefs. This discrepancy between how people **say** they would behave and their actual behaviour is not new.

Nor is it surprising that most people wind up living by the same set of irrational and unrealistic beliefs, since most of us have had broadly the same education. From birth onwards, we were taught by our parents to feel embarrassed, awkward and guilty about our sexual anatomy and explorations. We gather a load of misinformation from our peer groups, mainly via jokes and boasting. Broadly, boys are taught to see sexual prowess and accomplishments as major components of masculine success, and girls are taught a romanticised but sterilised view of sex.

Finally, most of us polish up all of this theory by attending the practical classes – we go petting. Petting, meaning deliberate sexual contact that does not include intercourse, is nearly a universal teenage experience. As the Kinsey studies showed, petting actually shows regular patterns of development and content. All that time you spent fogging up the car windows, or fumbling on the lounge, imagining that you were doing wicked, unthinkable things, it turns out that everybody else was doing much the same thing in much the same order. Sort of takes the romance out of life, doesn't it. Usually the guy takes the initiative, both in starting petting and choosing techniques. If the girl is active, it's in response to his initiative.

Petting is seen by both sexes as a prelude to intercourse. As you may remember, the aim of the game for the boy was to get the girl aroused enough to let her self-control slip far enough to let him go a bit further this time than last time. For her part, the aim of the game was to enjoy what he does to her, but not let herself get so aroused that they go 'all the way'.

These are powerful learning experiences. Both partners are acquiring a set of beliefs about sex that define active and passive roles, responsibility for sexual arousal and satisfaction, and the means of achieving these. It is these beliefs which we think set people up for sexual problems. The widespread nature of these beliefs, arising from our common sex education experiences, probably accounts for the widespread occurrence of sexual difficulties. We now expect to spend some time, in every sex counselling case, helping people see how they have been fooled into uncritically accepting these beliefs, and how the beliefs, however popular, are simply wrong.

You, too, may recognise how your sexual behaviour and relationships have been influenced by these beliefs. Read the next bit with an open mind. We're not asking you how much you agree with these beliefs. When they are written out in black and white, it's easy to see how silly they are. Rather, we're suggesting you ask yourself how much your sexual behaviour and relationships may have been influenced by such ideas, however unconsciously.

Myth Number 1

'Intercourse is the 'adult', 'best', 'most important' part of sex.'

Most adults will believe this myth, but it is an arbitrary, time- and culture-bound view of sexuality. By giving too much emphasis to intercourse, couples put pressure on the man to get and keep erections, and pressure on the woman to experience orgasm in intercourse whereas recent research shows this unlikely. This performance pressure on both partners can cause considerable difficulty for the man and disappointment for the woman. Few women find intercourse sufficiently physically arousing to have orgasm.

Myth Number 2

'Men take the initiative in sex.'

Both men and women often believe this, as a result of their shared petting experiences. But there is no logical or scientific reason for it being so, and believing this myth can again cause performance pressure on the man, and disappointment for the woman. If she is prepared to take as much initiative as he is, then she reduces the pressure on him, and can be more certain that sex will occur when and how she likes.

Myth Number 3

'The man is responsible for his partner's satisfaction as well as his own.'

Unfortunately, many couples believe this myth, resulting again in performance pressure on him and disappointment for her. It is our firm belief that each person is responsible for his or her own sexual satisfaction. It is not his or her partner's responsibility. At the very least, each person needs to know what kind of stimulation he or she likes, and then needs to take enough initiative during sexual activity to make sure that he or she gets that kind of stimulation. Research on the female orgasm has shown just how unimportant a contribution was made by the man's so-called expertise.

Myth Number 4

'Women are less interested in sex than men. They are slower to become sexually aroused and need more stimulation.'

Although many cultures have taught this myth, it has no scientific basis at all. Sexually responsive women are no less interested in sex than are sexually responsive men. And if the couple uses sexual techniques chosen by the woman as much as by the man, then she will respond just as quickly as he does.

Myth Number 5

'A man's penis is the best part of his body for stimulating his partner.'

Many cultures have placed great emphasis on the penis, and this results in some most unfortunate expectations. If you look at a penis its deficiencies as a stimulating device are apparent. It has two possible positions, up or down. It is attached between male hips which are rather inflexible. And it's a long way from your eyes, which makes it difficult to see what you're doing with it.

It is fine for a man to expect to enjoy **receiving** stimulation to his penis. It is unrealistic for him to expect to **give** much effective stimulation to his partner with his penis. He will expect this, of course, if he believes Myth No. 1, the 'importance' of intercourse. Other parts of his anatomy, such as his fingers and tongue, are far more effective at **giving** stimulation.

Myth Number 6

'A woman's vagina is the best part of her body for receiving sexual stimulation.'

This myth, like No. 5 above, is related to Myth No. 1. Unfortunately many people believe it, so many women begin to wonder what is wrong with them, because they do not find vaginal stimulation very arousing. In fact, research shows that vaginal stimulation is not highly physically arousing for most women, and few women will experience orgasm as a result of just intercourse. The clitoris is definitely the woman's most sexually responsive part, and most women need some more or less direct stimulation of the clitoris in order to experience orgasm. This can, of course, precede, accompany or follow intercourse, and a man doesn't need an erection to give clitoral stimulation.

Myth Number 7

'All good sex ends in orgasm. In really good sex, both partners have orgasm at the same time.'

These are popular myths, but are as untrue as the rest, and believing them also causes performance pressure on both partners. This pressure in turn causes sexual difficulty, including missed orgasm. Orgasms are an enjoyable part of sex, but are not essential for satisfaction. Coincidental orgasm is just that – a coincidence – and striving for it will simply reduce sexual satisfaction.

Myth Number 8

'Sex ends at fifty.'

Unfortunately, this myth has been supported in the past by well-intentioned but uninformed professionals. There are no medical or psychological reasons why a couple should not enjoy a mutually satisfactory sexual relationship throughout their lives together, barring the intrusion of physical effects (which can often be treated). Reduction in sexual interest and activity after fifty are usually due to ill-based expectations.

AN ALTERNATIVE VIEW OF SEX

In place of these myths, we suggest an alternative view of sex, which we think is more realistically based. We suggest that a sexual relationship is one in which both partners have orgasms most of the time, somehow or other. It doesn't matter what sexual techniques they use, so long as they are comfortable and acceptable for both partners. There are so many ways of expressing and sharing your sexuality that there is no need to over-emphasise any one sexual technique (such as intercourse), nor any need for either partner to put up with a sexual technique he or she doesn't really like. And, it doesn't matter which partner may sometimes not have orgasm, so long as they are both content that they have orgasms as often as they want.

Our conclusion is an anatomical revision. Your major sex organ is the one between your ears. If it is well-informed, reasonably comfortable and relaxed, then sex is usually fine. If it is ill-informed, uncomfortable or anxious, then you can do what you like to the rest of the body but sex probably won't be much good. The wonderful thing about the brain is that, throughout life, it remains flexible and able to learn new, more successful ways of behaving.

PRACTICAL EXERCISE

Discussing sexual myths

Set aside time for a discussion of the sex myths.
How much has your sexual relationship been influenced by these ideas?
What do you expect of your sexual relationship in the future?
Again, if you have major differences in your expectations, you may need to wait for Chapters 6 and 7 to resolve them.

SENSATE FOCUS

Because sensate focus has been used very successfully as part of the treatment of many sex problems, it has unfortunately come to be regarded as a bit of a panacea. We describe the sensate focus programme later in this section. It is often prescribed as a sexual cure-all, especially by inadequately trained 'sex therapists'. In fact, there are four prerequisites for successful sensate focus, and you should make sure you meet all four before going ahead with the programme.

Prerequisites for sensate focus

First, you need two motivated and co-operative partners. Both of you must have agreed that you want to improve your sexual relationship, and that you want to do the sensate focus programme for that reason. If one of you is unwilling or resentful, that will sabotage the programme and may even make it counter-productive.

If you don't meet this prerequisite, that strongly suggests that there are broader problems in your relationship, at least that there is major disagreement over the sexual relationship. You may be able to resolve this, using the procedures in Chapters 6 and 7.

Second, you both need to be reasonably assertive, at least within your relationship. The programme requires each of you to communicate to the other what you like and what you don't like. So, you have to be reasonably able to do that already. In our society, women in particular are taught to be submissive, and often have difficulty giving their sexual partners direct feedback or requests.

If either of you feels a lack of assertiveness, then you should tackle that problem first. Refer to the section later in this chapter on assertiveness.

Third, you should both have a reasonable degree of body comfort. That is, you need to feel reasonably comfortable with your partner looking at and touching your body, since that's basically what sensate focus involves. If one of you isn't comfortable about his or her body, it's possible that the graded approach built into sensate focus may help you overcome that discomfort, especially if the other partner is supportive. You can start your sensate focus programme clothed, at least in a gown of some kind, and with the lights off, and gradually increase your nakedness and the light level. But if this is a serious problem, some professional assistance may be indicated.

Fourth, you need sufficient time, and a place with privacy. If your sexual relationship has real priority for you, then that should be expressed in your willingness to set aside two or three times a week to do your sensate focus programme. Privacy and freedom from intrusion are important to create the relaxed atmosphere necessary for the programme to work best.

For some couples, this prerequisite is difficult to meet because of other commitments, kids, and so on. But it has been our experience that genuinely motivated couples can overcome these obstacles. Couples who come up with a string of semi-plausible excuses for not doing their sensate focus are often really saying they don't want to work on the programme or their sexual relationship.

If you and your partner agree that you meet these four prerequisites, you are ready for sensate focus. You should first read and discuss the programme, and then agree when you are going to start.

Aims of sensate focus

There are four aims to the sensate focus programme. Understanding these can help you to get more out of the programme by helping you to understand why it is done as we have described it below. It is important that you follow the programme as described.

First, sensate focus helps to reduce performance anxiety,

which is the thing that most often inhibits sexual arousal. The more you worry about your sexual performance, the more anxious you feel, and the less you respond. In sensate focus there are none of the usual goals or arbitrary standards that can intrude into everyday sex: he doesn't have to get an erection; she doesn't have to lubricate; no-one has to have an orgasm; you only have to be willing to share pleasure.

Second, sensate focus systematically challenges the popular myth of the primacy of intercourse. An over-emphasis on intercourse is one of the most common causes of sexual dissatisfaction and difficulty. By forbidding intercourse until its third stage, sensate focus helps you get intercourse into perspective, as a part of sex but not necessarily the most important or enjoyable part.

Third, by systematically guiding you through exploration of each other's sensuality and sexuality, sensate focus aids the development of a broad and varied sexual relationship. Eventually you will have a range of sexual techniques to draw on, so that each sexual occasion includes some sexual stimulation that each finds arousing and that both find comfortable. This store of information about how to give each other sexual pleasure becomes your insurance against future sexual boredom.

And fourth, the nature of the programme helps you build up habits of open, direct and comfortable communication about sex. Good communication is an essential ingredient of a successful, long-term sexual relationship. It is not sufficient by itself, as has sometimes been suggested, but it is necessary. Sexual likes and dislikes vary amongst people, and for the one person on different occasions. The only way for your partner to know what you want or don't want is for you to communicate that.

As we said above, only you can take responsibility for your own sexual satisfaction. The minimum requirement is that you communicate with your partner, so that what happens in sex is comfortable for both of you, and includes techniques arousing for each of you.

The basic programme

Sensate focus consists of a series of pleasuring sessions, during each of which one partner gives the other tactile pleasure.

Pleasuring can include touching, stroking, tickling, massaging, licking, kissing or whatever is comfortable to both of you.

The partner who is being pleasured must give the other partner feedback on how he or she feels in response to being pleasured. This can be verbal – 'I like that', 'Up a bit, left a bit, harder, softer', 'I don't like that' – or it can be non-verbal – you can put your hand on your partner's hand and show him or her exactly where and how you like to be pleasured.

The partner who is giving pleasure must listen to this feedback. Learn about your partner's sensual and sexual responsiveness. Store away for future use what you learn about what gives your partner pleasure.

You can toss a coin to see who gives and who receives pleasure first. In your next session, swap roles. You can swap roles within a session, but be careful that you are both having roughly equal times in both roles, and you aren't bringing into sensate focus old habits of one partner doing most of the work.

To see progress, you should aim at having two or three sessions a week. Less will get you there, but slowly. The length of a session depends on pleasure and comfort. As soon as either one of you gets bored or feels anxious or uncomfortable, you say: 'I would like to stop now' (**not** 'Have you had enough'). You are better off having a good ten minutes than a protracted half an hour, although generally sessions last for about 30 to 60 minutes.

The programme goes through three major stages:

Stage 1: In this stage you pleasure each other anywhere on the body, except on the genitals and, no matter how aroused you may become, you don't have intercourse. From this stage you will discover, or rediscover, how much pleasure you can give to each other, without ever having intercourse, and without it even being a very sexual exercise. This stage is important for couples who feel their relationship is lacking in physical expression of affection.

Stage 2: This stage includes everything you did in Stage 1, and you can now add direct pleasuring of each other's genitals. Still, no matter how aroused you become, you should not have intercourse. Many people really don't know how the other sex likes to be stimulated, and often assume their partner will like the same stimulation as they do. Everyone is individual, and changing, in what they like. This stage is your chance to teach each other exactly how you like to be aroused. It is also an opportunity to learn how satisfying sex can be, without even having intercourse.

Stage 3: In this final stage of sensate focus, you include all of the pleasuring you have discovered in the first two stages, and you can now add intercourse. Usually you begin this with the woman on top, sitting on her partner, but from there you should explore positions with the usual proviso: what you do should be enjoyable and comfortable for both partners.

You should note that each of the later stages includes what was done in the earlier stages. It doesn't replace them so that you again wind up with a sexual relationship which consists only of intercourse.

You have as many sessions as you like at each stage, until you meet two goals. First, you both feel comfortable with everything you want to do at this stage. And second, you both feel you have learned all there is to know about giving your partner pleasure at that stage. It doesn't matter whether you take two or ten sessions to achieve these goals. Sensate focus is not a race. You are better off taking a bit longer to get through the programme, and getting all of the benefit possible, than hurrying through and missing out on the benefit.

Tips for successful sensate focus

If it's your turn to be pleasured, give information to your partner. Use 'I' messages, such as 'I like that' or 'I don't like that'. Pleased grunts and groans will do. Don't expect your partner to read your mind, use communication skills.

If it's your turn to give pleasure, listen to your partner. Don't use 'you' messages, such as 'You don't like this, do you'. Accept that your partner is the world's only expert on his or her feelings. 'You' messages are mind-reading, and research shows that this is often wrong. Use your communication skills.

Don't let old demands, goals or pressure intrude. The man

does not have to get or keep an erection; the woman does not have to lubricate; no-one has to have an orgasm. You only have to give and receive pleasure, and communicate about that.

Stick to the programme. Sometimes people will make what they think is a small change to a programme, but in fact it has a major effect on the programme. Many failures in self-help come from not following the programme.

Expect to feel awkward and embarrassed, at least at the beginning, especially if your sexual relationship has got a bit rusty. It does seem silly to have to take a printed guide to bed – 'Excuse me, dear, I just have to turn the page' – but recognise that sensate focus is a structured learning programme.

Once you have mastered the skills that come from sensate focus, you can use them spontaneously and naturally, within your improved sexual relationship. But for now, you are learning. Don't confuse your sexual enhancement programme with your sexual relationship.

If sex is still OK for both of you at present, continue your sexual relationship at other times. If sex has become a negative experience for one of you, it's better to call a halt on sex until sensate focus has proceeded far enough for positive feelings to return.

If you get sexually frustrated because you are aroused during an early session of sensate focus when you should not have intercourse, we suggest you masturbate. If you cheat on the programme, you only cheat yourself.

Use a lubricant to make pleasuring more comfortable and sensual. We suggest baby oil: it's readily obtained, aesthetically pleasant, and washes out of bed clothes. Warm a little in your hands, and then spread it on your partner's body. If you don't like baby oil, try massage oil, moisturing lotions, or talcum powder.

Having a bath or shower beforehand can help you both feel comfortable being close; doing it together can start the mood. One or two drinks (but no more) can also help you to relax. If you're feeling lavish, sip some champagne as you go. Appropriate music and lighting can also set the scene.

PRACTICAL EXERCISE
Sensate focus

Read and discuss the information above about the sensate focus programme. Agree when you will start, and hop into it!

Keep sensate focus in mind as a coping skill you can use anytime you feel your sexual relationship is flagging and needs a boost.

SEXUAL ASSERTIVENESS

Assertiveness training has become something of a bandwagon lately, with a growing number of courses being offered by people of rather varying expertise. Unfortunately some of these courses boil down to giving participants permission to be rude and aggressive, which shows how little their leaders know about real assertiveness.

Even many of the good ones focus on particular areas, such as how to be more assertive on the job, or when dealing with salesmen, or making complaints. These are good areas to look at, relevant for many people, but they omit some common problem areas such as intimate relationships, particularly sexual ones.

A good sexual relationship is one in which the partners use sexual techniques which are acceptable and comfortable to both, including some which will be arousing and satisfying for each of them. Being able to say, comfortably and directly, what you want and don't want, and when, is sexual assertiveness.

Given that our society still tends to train women to be submissive, it's not surprising that many of them are not very sexually assertive. Women will often put up with their partners' choice of sexual technique, even though they may find it basically unexciting, or even unpleasant. For some time this has been recognised by a growing number of women, and women's sexual assertiveness groups are springing up, and other women's groups will often discuss issues of sexual assertiveness.

Just as the whole of male liberation and men's consciousness-raising lags behind its female counterpart, so does the idea that men might benefit from sexual assertiveness training. In fact, we think they have at least as much to gain as the women.

Many people will tell us that they don't have an assertiveness problem; they are already quite assertive. That's good, we'll agree, suppose you show us how you would assertively handle someone who was offending you. They then unleash a wild, aggressive attack which, they assure us, really put the other person in his box.

Confusion between assertiveness and aggression is common. As we'll explain shortly, there is a gigantic difference, but many people are unaware of it.

Men in our culture are taught to be aggressive rather than assertive. We think this applies especially to the sexual area, where men are trained throughout adolescence that they must take the sexual initiative, they are responsible for choosing the sexual techniques, and if a woman says 'No' she means 'Not yet'.

The first fundamental assumption of assertiveness training is that assertiveness, rather than aggression, manipulation or submission, enriches your life and leads to more satisfying relationships. The sexual corollary of this is that sexual assertiveness leads to more mutually satisfying and rewarding sexual relationships.

So we thought it would be of interest and potential value to both men and women if we considered the topic of assertiveness, with particular reference to sexual assertiveness. A brief discussion like this is never of great practical help, although we'll suggest some steps and resources. But it may encourage you to look for more.

Assertiveness is a practical skill, so it's easiest learned by watching someone demonstrate it, and then practising it yourself with some corrective feedback. This is what goes on in assertiveness courses. If you balk at the idea of doing a course, some good self-help references are: *The Assertive Option* by P. Jakubowski & A. Lange (Research Press); *Your Perfect Right* by R. Alberti & M. Emmons (Impact Publishers); and *The Assertive Woman* by S. Phelps &

N. Austin (also Impact Publishers). The last has a chapter on sexual assertiveness.

If you decide to try to increase your sexual assertiveness, in a steady relationship, it's a good idea to involve your partner. Read and discuss this section together, for starters. If one of the partners in a relationship starts to become more assertive, that can rock the relationship boat and cause more strife than good.

What is assertiveness?

Essentially assertiveness means standing up for your rights, and expressing your thoughts, feelings, beliefs and wishes in direct, honest and appropriate ways, which respect the rights of others. Sexual assertiveness means expressing your sexual wishes and feelings clearly and directly, while respecting the wishes and feelings of your partner.

In contrast, there are two broad forms of non-assertion: aggression and submission.

Aggression is self-expression which violates the rights of others, and demeans others in an attempt to achieve your own aims. The typical motivation for being aggressive is an underlying fear of losing power or control in the situation, which in turn often reflects a basic lack of self-confidence.

Sexual aggression not only includes the obvious inflicting of your sexual wishes on someone else by force, but also the more subtle emotional manipulations intended to coerce your partner into accepting sex, or a sexual technique, against his or her real wishes.

Submissiveness involves behaviour which violates your own rights, by failing to express your thoughts, feelings or wishes honestly. The typical motives for being submissive are underlying fears of losing the approval of others or of eliciting hostile reactions, but it also sometimes results from being confused with politeness.

In a sexual context, submissiveness may involve giving in to your partner's requests for sex, or for a particular sexual technique, when you don't really want it; or it may involve not asking for sex, or for a particular sexual technique, when you really do want it.

Becoming more assertive

Becoming more assertive involves:

1 Recognising the differences between assertion, aggression, submission and politeness.

2 Identifying and accepting your personal rights, and the rights of others.

3 Changing thoughts and coping with feelings that stop you from being assertive.

4 Developing your assertive skills by actively practising them.

Identifying assertiveness

Read through the definitions above of assertiveness, aggression and submission. Responsible assertiveness involves flexibility, being able to look at each situation afresh and decide how genuinely important to you are the issues involved.

If you disagree with someone else's views or actions, but it isn't really important to you if they think or act that way, you may say nothing. In the context of intimate relationships, we call this editing: getting your petty complaints into perspective and editing out the unimportant ones.

On the other hand, if the issue is genuinely important to you, then you should speak up, or you are being submissive. Of course, you should speak up assertively, not aggressively.

If you are enhancing your assertiveness by self-help, you can practise picking assertion, aggression and submission by watching the interactions of those around you, and deciding which behaviour was involved each time. Assertive people can be a good source of examples for you: if they can do it, so can you!

Unless you are into voyeurism, this learning-by-observation may be a bit difficult for specifically sexual situations, although you might try a few R-rated movies, and even the flirting and sexual horseplay that go on in many social situations will do.

Identifying your rights

The second fundamental assumption underlying assertiveness training is that everyone is entitled to act assertively and to express honest thoughts, feelings and beliefs. This is even more of an assumption than the first one; there is plenty of support for the notion that assertiveness is a successful interpersonal style.

But the idea that everyone should be allowed to be assertive is a flat assumption, a value judgment that you either accept or don't. It may look a self-evident truth to you, but there are still plenty of instances where people, consciously or unconsciously, question the right of women to be assertive, and the idea often hasn't even been considered for groups like children or employees.

If you don't believe that both partners in an intimate relationship have equal rights, then sexual assertiveness isn't for you.

For most of us, the major obstacle to accepting personal rights is our history of being socialised to accept ideas which deny them. Common socialisation messages that most of us grew up with include: 'Don't be selfish', 'Be modest and humble', 'Be understanding', 'Don't be demanding' and 'Don't hurt other people'.

Of course, there is some wisdom or justice in each of these ideas; the problem lies in their exaggeration. Against them, we encourage people to be reasonably self-centred because we believe you must look out for, appreciate, stand up for and express yourself, before you can do anything really worthwhile for others. Martyrs are a pain in the neck who often do more harm than good.

Our sexual socialisation doesn't help assertiveness, either. Growing up under the double standard, as we mentioned earlier, broadly teaches men to be sexually aggressive and women to be sexually passive. Men often do wind up believing they have both the right and the duty to take all the sexual initiatives, as is shown by the growing awareness of the extent of sexual harassment in the workplace. Paradoxically, within a sexual relationship many men are reluctant to ask their partners for a particular sexual technique because this would imply passivity and dependence on the part of the man.

Women often do wind up believing they have neither the right nor the need to take any sexual initiatives, as is partly evidenced by the massive extent of women's dissatisfaction with their sexual responses. Relying on their partners' mythical male expertise for their sexual arousal and satisfaction, many women wind up believing they are 'frigid' when they are only uninformed.

We emphasise to couples that only one person can take responsibility for your sexual satisfaction, and that's you. Even if you choose to be relatively physically passive on any sexual occasion, you have to be mentally active, focussing on your sexual feelings or fantasies to enhance your arousal, and you have to communicate to your partner what you want and don't want. A good sexual partner is not a trick bag of dazzling sexual technique, but someone who looks for and is guided by feedback as to what you want and don't want. He or she can contribute to your sexual satisfaction by this willingness, but cannot take over your responsibility for it. And that involves being sexually assertive.

Changing thoughts and coping with feelings

Ideally, you should identify which of your own thoughts and feelings are hindering your sexual assertiveness. And then challenge the rationality of the thoughts and recognise that you can cope with the feelings, that they are not really important barriers to better sexuality. Here are some examples of how to do this for some common interfering thoughts and feelings. Try to adapt them to you.

If you think you are unnecessarily sexually aggressive, because you are afraid of letting your partner take control, practise this self-talk:

'I know I may feel anxious when I stop trying to control our sexual interactions, but I can cope with feeling anxious, and it's important to me that we share the sexual initiative and responsibility so that sex is really good for both of us. So I'll relax as much as I can and give it a try.'

If you think you are unnecessarily sexually submissive because you are frightened of your partner's reactions if you were more assertive, practise this self-talk:

'I know I may feel anxious when I refuse a sexual request (or when I make a sexual request), and I would feel bad if my partner reacted badly, but I can cope with those bad feelings. I have as many sexual rights as my partner, and it's important for me that I express them, so here I go.'

If new self-talk like this would be appropriate for you, it helps to write it on a small card, and carry it around, rehearsing it until you can automatically think more rationally when you are in a sexual situation. It could be a bit clumsy if you have to interrupt sex for a refresher course.

Developing assertive skills

Once you have a reasonably clear idea of what would be more sexually assertive behaviour for you, the next step is to try it out. Set yourself some clear goals, but do it in gradual steps. There is no such thing as trial-and-error learning: failures discourage people and cause them to stop trying.

People learn by succeeding. Success encourages you, so you keep trying and keep progressing. Effective behaviour change programmes use the principle of taking small steps, one at a time. If being sexually assertive is a long way from where you are now, work your way there gradually and successfully.

Some examples of sexually assertive behaviours are:

Telling your partner how you feel about something he or she does:
'When you do X, in situation Y, I feel Z.'
For example:
'When you stroke my breasts softly, while you kiss the nipples, I feel nice and tingly.'
or, 'When you rub my penis hard, before it's really erect, I feel uncomfortable.'

You may want to accompany this verbal feedback with a request for something different:
For example:
'I would like gentle stimulation more, until I'm erect.'

Other verbal assertiveness can include making clear sexual requests:
For example:
'I would like to make love with me on top this time.'

And asking your partner what he or she would like. As we said before, a good sexual partner is willing to listen to and be guided by this sort of sexual communication.

Sexual communication doesn't have to be, and often isn't, verbal. For example, you can give your partner good assertive feedback by moving his or her hand to where you would like to be touched, or guiding them as to how you would like to be touched.

Any time you are trying to behave more sexually assertively, and you are being hindered by feeling anxious or uncertain, use the self-talk suggested above.

5
Fight control skills

'You never do anything I ask. You always think of yourself first.'
'Well, what about you last week! You sat around all day while I did the cleaning up and then you always pick on what I've done.'
'I'm fed up! You're just a lazy so-and-so and I can't stand you any longer.'
'Well if that's the way you feel, I'm leaving.'
(Exits slamming the door.)

We hope after reading our chapter on communication, and working through the exercises, that you recognise the very poor communication that occurred in this dialogue.

For many couples learning and practising good communication skills are important steps in reducing the number of disagreements that lead to arguments. However, being able to use these skills in heated moments can sometimes be difficult. In this chapter, we will outline fight control skills, some practical steps you can take to cut down on fighting and make it easier to use your communication and problem-solving skills.

As we said before, this chapter may not be necessary for all couples. It obviously is necessary for couples who are arguing a lot. If conflict has become a central part of your relationship, you will probably need to work through this chapter early in your programme. Otherwise, you may find it difficult even to begin the other exercises and you may fall into the trap, discussed before, of using the programme as something more to fight over.

WIZARD OF ID   COPYRIGHT FIELD NEWSPAPER SYNDICATE

But a simple lack of fights doesn't mean you won't benefit from working on your fight control skills. A low rate of arguing can mean the couple have few issues to argue about, presumably because they can usually resolve differences satisfactorily. But it can also mean that their unsatisfactory attempts to resolve issues in the past, usually by fighting, have been so distressing for both of them that they have simply learned to avoid contentious issues.

What do you think? If you haven't had many fights lately, is that because you haven't much to fight about, or because you have decided it's better just to 'let sleeping dogs lie'?

The difficulty for the latter approach is that now, when you are practising and using your communication skills, you will no longer be able to ignore or pretend away the hot issues in your relationship. In fact, we strongly discourage you from doing that. Ignored problems don't go away; they often get worse because they are being ignored.

Even if you have never argued, or not for a long time, if there is a chance of your doing so when you finally discuss the main problems in your relationship, then you should first work your way through this chapter. Above all, recognise that it takes two of you, not only to fight, but also to stop fighting.

As we said in Chapter 1, fights are always destructive. They chip away at the good faith each of you has in the relationship, and in each other's intentions towards it and feelings towards each other. You will not gain much from implementing the other relationship skills – coupling, communication and so on – if you are continually under-cutting your gains in those areas by creating mutual ill-feeling and mistrust through fighting.

Let us repeat our warning, especially for couples who tend to fight. **Do not** let disagreements over the instructions in this manual become another issue to fight over. Many couples who come to therapy because of their fighting, try to use therapy as another issue for arguments. This is destructive and reduces any chance of beginning to change for the better.

If you continue to argue frequently, even after trying to follow the guidelines in this chapter, we recommend that you seek assistance from a properly qualified clinical psychologist.

Now let us give you some practical advice on fight control. This falls into two broad groups: skills for each of you to use as individuals, and skills for both of you to use together.

INDIVIDUAL FIGHT CONTROL SKILLS

Tracking your own arousal

The more upset you are, the harder it is to think or act sensibly, including making deliberate use of your relationship skills. Yet only you can reliably tell how upset you are, and when you are getting close to losing your temper. So this must be an individual responsibility, and tracking your own level of arousal is an individual skill. Doing it becomes an individual contribution each should make to the relationship.

Many arguments occur, or escalate, because people are unaware of the point at which they become too angry to continue a discussion in any reasonable way. For example, he will continue the discussion even though he looks like thunder, his voice is becoming louder, he is clenching his fists, his face is red, he is leaning forward and thumping the table very aggressively and his communication has slipped into accusations.

Meanwhile, she is responding to his non-verbal behaviour and becoming angry also. She begins raising her voice, pointing aggressively, clenching her teeth, getting red in the face and throwing accusations back in a sniping manner.

The signs of anger in this couple are obvious to anybody, probably even to themselves, in the end. But there would usually have been many warning signs before they reached this level of conflict, signs which they have either ignored or not even been aware of.

These early warning signs, because they occur before you are very upset, are the best signals of your need to do something constructive **before** the situation escalates into a full-blown argument. It is much easier to act sensibly when you are only feeling 5/10 annoyed than when you are feeling 10/10 furious.

What have you noticed in yourself? What are your early warning signs? Do you clench your fists or your teeth? Do you breathe faster, or talk louder and faster? Do you interrupt the other person? Do you have thoughts like, 'Here we go again'?

Many people have difficulty recognising their early warning signs. This isn't surprising when you consider how Anglo-Saxon culture teaches us not to recognise or deal with feelings. When you were growing up, how often were you told, 'Don't get angry!' or 'You shouldn't feel upset over something little like that!'

Now you can recognise these responses as showing a lack of validating in the person who said them. At the time, they probably made you feel worse. But they also taught you to hide your bad feelings, even from yourself.

Example

Alice found it very difficult to notice when she was angry with someone, particularly when she was angry with her husband. Yet she found it annoying that her husband left all the organisation of the house and children to her. She had her own job, and so found it very difficult to keep up with all of the demands on her.

Although she was sometimes aware of feeling bad about the situation, she would try to dismiss this to herself, because she saw herself as an 'intelligent person' who 'ought to be able to cope'. She especially did not want to nag her husband.

But every now and then, a series of things would go wrong at her work, and that evening she would suddenly find herself shouting at her husband over an issue which later she would recognise as trivial. Even that recognition would only make her feel worse – 'How could I get so upset over something so small!' – and even more inclined to deny bad feelings in the future.

Unfortunately, her husband didn't help matters. He would

notice Alice was not feeling good on these occasions, but would try to ignore her early warning signs, in the hope that it would all blow over before it blew up. This generally made him so tense that, by the time Alice started shouting, he was ready to shout back.

Their fights never got anywhere, basically because they were over unimportant issues that were just the last straw, not the real cause of their conflict. So both would feel frustrated, and pessimistic about the future of the relationship.

In this atmosphere, Alice would try all the harder not to feel bad. Which really meant she would bottle up more bad feelings, eventually to let them go in the next blow up. Obviously, they would have been better off if she had chosen to level about her bad feelings, whenever they occurred, or if her husband had at least invited her to level when she looked upset (see Chapter 3).

But she couldn't level, even if she had known how, about feelings she wasn't aware of herself. The trouble with trying to ignore bad feelings is that you don't recognise them early enough to handle them sensibly. You are more likely to **act** on them first, and then realise how bad you were feeling.

You can act out your bad feelings by screaming, by crashing objects on the floor, by sulking, by slamming doors, by snapping at your partner, by 'forgetting' to do something, by stopping your partner from doing something she enjoys, and so on. Later you may realise the feelings you were expressing non-verbally, but in the meantime you have probably antagonised or frightened your partner and damaged your relationship.

Accepting responsibility for how you feel, and therefore for how to change it

Once you are able to pick up the early warning signs that you are becoming so upset that an argument is becoming likely, you can then do something constructive to stop it. Some of what you can do involves both of you, and is described later. Here we want to explain how each of you can bring your own escalating feelings under better control.

Let's extend some of what we have already been saying about self-talk. How you feel about anything is largely determined by how you think about it. If you are feeling very angry or upset about something that your partner did, that is largely because of how you choose to think about it. And that's your responsibility.

Of course, your partner **influences** how you feel, because some of your thoughts and feelings are in response to what he does. But he does not **control** your thoughts, and therefore he does not **control** your feelings. You do.

Equally, if your partner (or anybody else) does something very aggressive or unfair to you, it is quite reasonable for you to feel angry. The question is how you express that reasonable anger: constructively – using relationship skills like communication and problem solving – or destructively – hitting back and escalating the argument?

It will be much easier for you to choose to act constructively if you can contain your anger to a reasonable level, rather than exaggerate it to yourself through unrealistic and irrational self-talk. The first step in doing this is to identify your own self-talk that is leading to your own bad feelings.

You are now ready to begin to identify your bad feelings, the self-talk that leads to them, how you express them, and which situations they occur in. From this information, you will be able to plan a strategy for handling your bad feelings better.

PRACTICAL EXERCISE

Analysing your own bad feelings

You need to begin by challenging the idea that there is something wrong with feeling bad. Give yourself permission to be human and feel bad sometimes. Recognise that in all relationships, no matter how good the relationship is, you will at times feel bad.

Second, notice that feeling bad does not lead to disastrous consequences, you just feel bad. Ask yourself how often in the last week you have felt bad. Do you still have two arms, two legs, head? Are you still able to make friends, work, pursue hobbies? The worst thing about feeling bad is that you feel bad. It is not the end of the world.

Sit down with a piece of paper and pen. Spend time writing out what **you** do when you are angry, upset, hurt, disappointed, sad. How do you feel physically: tense in the stomach, clenched teeth, tensed muscles? How do you behave: yell, sulk, work furiously, shut yourself off from others, pick on your partner? This exercise may not be all that easy. You may be very practised at ignoring how you feel.

Over the next week, start recording any significant feelings you have. For example, when Mary did this, her diary for the week looked like this:

Day	Situation	Feeling
Mon.	David arrived late home from work.	Angry
Tues.	Neighbour asked if I would take kids to school when I was busy.	Resentful
Wed.	Unable to go to David's work party.	Disappointed
Thurs.	David left me to mind kids while he went out.	Angry
Sun.	No-one helped me around the house.	Fed-up

Peter's record looked like this:

Day	Situation	Feeling
Mon.	Kids screaming when I got home.	Tired, irritable
Tues.	Anne yelling at the kids	Angry
Wed.	Anne went out without discussing the arrangements with me.	Upset
Thurs.	A bad day at work.	Tired, disappointed

In your diary you can now include a third piece of information. How do you act when you feel bad? Spend another week recording in your diary. You may find it easier to note your reaction and work backwards to how you feel, and then to the situation that triggered that feeling.

Day	Situation	Feeling	Reaction
Mon.	An argument with Dennis on Sunday.	Bad	Couldn't concentrate all day.
Tues.	Upset over work.	Upset	Snapped at Dennis when he spoke to me.
Sat.	Dennis went off to football.	Angry	Yelled at kids.
Sun.	Still angry.	Furious	Didn't speak to Dennis all day.
Tues.	Another argument with Dennis.	Upset, disappointed	Moped around all day.
Fri.	Repairman didn't turn up on time.	Frustrated, rushed	Snapped at Dennis for no reason.

Now add another column to your diary. This time we want you to take note of the situation, how you feel, your thoughts and reactions.

Day	Situation	Feeling	Thoughts	Reaction
Tues.	Louise forgot to post an important letter.	Angry	She did that on purpose. She never remembers to do things for me.	Left house and slammed door.
Fri.	Louise was late for our dinner engagement.	Frustrated, hurt	Why can't she be on time? She is always late.	Sulked at dinner.
Sun.	Louise did not consider my feelings.	Upset	She is always selfish and only thinks of herself.	Refused to play tennis with her.
Mon.	Bad day at the office.	Tired	She gets on my nerves. Can't she see that I am tired.	Snapped at Louise.

Another example:

Day	Situation	Feelings	Thoughts	Reaction
Thurs.	Greg drove over rubbish bin.	Annoyed	That fool, he never watches where he is going.	Yelled at Greg.
Fri.	Greg didn't notice the special meal I cooked.	Upset	Who does he think I am? He treats me like a slave.	Withdrew.
Sat.	Still felt bad after last night	Hurt	Sometimes I just feel like giving up. Why do I bother?	Moped around all morning.

You and your partner should have each begun to learn about your own feelings, your thoughts, and your reactions in distressing situations. You should both continue keeping your diaries until you feel that you are able to identify fairly easily how you feel, what you say to yourself under those circumstances and how you react when you are angry, upset, hurt or whatever.

Feeling better by thinking straighter and acting constructively

From the above exercise, you should have identified some of your self-talk that increases your degree of upset. Sometimes it's obvious, because you can easily see how unreasonable and how unrealistic your thoughts are. That's good, because shortly we'll show you how to deal with those thoughts.

But sometimes it's much harder to get in touch with your self-talk. This is particularly true for thoughts you have practised so often that they have become 'automatic'.

To understand this idea of an automatic thought, think of a habit you have, such as running your hands through your hair or sitting a certain way. These habits will seem to occur automatically, because you have practised them so much that you are mostly unaware of doing them.

You may become aware of a habit if someone points it out to you, but generally we do not notice our own habits. This is usually helpful. Your mind would be very busy indeed if it had to keep close track of everything you were doing all of the time. By developing habits, we are able to let our routine behaviours take care of themselves, so that our minds can devote themselves more fully to new or difficult tasks. Thoughts are behaviours like any others, except that they happen inside your head. Like other behaviours, some thoughts can become habits and so occur without your really being aware of them.

This does not mean that these automatic, habitual thoughts are not under your control, any more than your other habits cannot be controlled by you. It does mean that the first step in exercising control over your automatic thoughts is to become aware of them. Your bad feelings diary should have helped you to do that.

Sometimes people have practised their automatic thoughts so much that they have disappeared completely from awareness. Now it seems that a particular situation, like your partner coming home late (again!), immediately produces bad feelings in you, without any thoughts at all on your part.

This is understandable. Remember when you were learning to drive (or to do some similarly complicated task), the loud conversations you had with yourself, inside your head. 'Now, push this pedal down, and move the gear stick over there, turn the wheel, whoops, check in the mirror!' and so on.

Once you have practised driving a lot, those conscious thoughts seem to disappear – you can talk to a passenger in the car, or listen to the radio – but they were there as a part of learning to drive. You will notice they come back when you are suddenly required to cope with a new driving situation, like visiting a country where they drive on the other side of the road.

This is just one example of a more general process. Humans use their thoughts to guide their reactions – feelings and behaviours – to new situations, including those in their relationships. If you experience the same situation many times, the thoughts may seem to disappear, but they were there at the beginning, and they are the essential path to changing your reactions, both feelings and behaviours.

This is such a universal process in human behaviour that we spend a lot of time in therapy with people for all kinds of problems, helping them to recognise how their self-talk contributes to the problem, and how to change their self-talk as part of the solution to the problem.

We have found this is a vital part of relationship therapy, so we will now outline the steps for you. Here we have explained them in terms of improving your relationship, but you should recognise that you can use these steps to cope better with bad feelings coming from any part of your life.

How to handle bad feelings better

Step 1: Get in touch with your feelings This may not be as easy as it looks if you have practised denying your feelings. In our culture, men are especially trained to deny bad feelings like anxiety or helplessness, while women are especially trained to deny bad feelings like anger or aggression. Your bad feelings diary is a systematic way of doing this step, and leads on to the later ones.

Be careful to record feelings (e.g. sad, anxious, angry,

frustrated) and not thoughts (e.g. 'I felt that I was being put down', or 'I felt as if I wasn't getting anywhere'); we'll get to the thoughts next.

It can also be helpful to record how strong the feeling was for you, as a percentage of possible feeling strength. Mild annoyance might be 10 per cent while being nearly as angry as you ever could be might be 95 per cent. This estimate of how bad you are feeling at the beginning of the exercise gives you a mark from which to measure your progress.

Everybody feels bad sometimes, and that's desirable and healthy. If you miss out on something you had your heart set on, you ought to feel disappointed. If your partner does something mean to you, you ought to feel hurt. Trying to deny bad feelings not only doesn't get rid of them, it often makes them worse.

But it's equally self-defeating to exaggerate your bad feelings, as many of us have learned to do. Exaggerated bad feelings make us feel worse than is reasonable and often disrupt our behaviour so that we are less successful than we could have been. Making yourself furious, by thinking unrealistically, over some trivial incident in your relationship hurts you, by making you upset, and your relationship, by making you act out aggressively.

It is these exaggerated bad feelings that are the target of this procedure. Our aim is to accept reasonable bad feelings, not to deny them, but also not to exaggerate them. Recording the original strength of your feeling allows you to see how you are reducing it to a reasonable level.

For example:

'Monday night: Felt 80 per cent disappointed when I came home and Jill didn't ask me how my day had gone.'

Step 2: Listen to your self-talk Listen to your thoughts about the situation. What are you saying to yourself that makes you feel so bad? Look for the thoughts that are obviously linked to your feelings.

Continuing our example:

'She really doesn't care how hard I work, as long as she has all the money she wants to spend. She never shows any interest in my job. She makes me feel unimportant around here.'

As we said above, you may have practised your reaction to a situation so much that you are no longer able to pick up what your original thoughts were. Don't worry – if you can't detect your self-talk leading to your bad feelings in a particular situation, just skip the next step and go straight to Step 4.

Step 3: Test your self-talk The trouble with automatic thoughts is that, because you hardly notice them any more, you uncritically accept them as 100 per cent true. And then, quite logically, you feel very bad. The point is, if you are feeling very bad, that will usually mean your self-talk is unrealistic or irrational, at least to some extent. It is this unrealistic flavour to your thoughts that causes the exaggeration of your feelings.

So, the purpose of this step is to get you to stop just accepting your automatic thoughts as 100 per cent true, and instead to test them as if they were little theories about the situation. Ask yourself, what evidence is there that my self-talk is true? How realistic are my thoughts? How reasonable am I being?

Sometimes what you have recorded for your self-talk will seem to be completely accurate, not unrealistic at all. Yet you are still feeling very bad. This usually means that, in addition to the self-talk you have recorded, there was another implicit thought: 'And it's dreadful that the world is like this!'

Continuing our example:

> 'It is disappointing she hasn't asked about my day, but maybe there's a good reason for that. I don't know for a fact that she doesn't care about my work. We have sometimes had good discussions about it. How I feel is finally my responsibility, so I'll level with her now.'

Step 4: Replace your self-talk with a coping self-statement It's not enough to recognise that what you have been saying to yourself is unrealistic, if not downright silly. That sometimes makes people feel worse, 'Gee, I must be stupid to think like that'.

It is replacing your unrealistic self-talk with more realistic self-talk that makes an immediate difference to your feelings.

Step 3 begins that replacement process. This step completes it, by giving you a different set of thoughts to use in the situation.

If you have been able to catch your original self-talk, in Step 2, and then test it in Step 3, you can now replace it with the coping self-statement below. If you couldn't find your self-talk in Step 2, and you have come straight to this step, that's fine. Just start to practise the coping self-statement, too. Here it is:

> 'I expect to feel (bad) (in this situation), but I can cope with that feeling. I don't have to deny my feelings, but I don't have to exaggerate them, either. If possible, I will do something constructive to improve the situation. If that's not possible, I'm not going to make myself feel worse than is reasonable.'

There are three key ideas in this self-statement: giving yourself permission to have reasonable bad feelings, because you can cope with them; not exaggerating them through irrational thinking or self-defeating behaviour; and doing something constructive, if that's possible.

By 'cope', we mean survive. There are no terminal cases of bad feelings. How many times in your life have you felt bad? But your arms haven't dropped off, nor your legs collapsed, nor anything else bad happened directly as a result of feeling bad. Bad feelings are unpleasant – we don't want to deny that – but that's all they are. We can all cope with feeling bad.

You can fit this general purpose coping self-statement to any situation, by simply putting in the appropriate bad feeling and situation. Then practise it in your head over and over again. If it is possible, do something constructive, like using your relationship skills.

Continuing our example:

> 'I expect to feel disappointed when Jill doesn't ask me how my day has gone, but I can cope with feeling disappointed. I don't have to deny feeling disappointed, but I won't exaggerate it, either. Now, what can I do that's constructive? I know, I'll level with her about how I'm feeling, and ask her to show more interest in the future.'

Now, how are you feeling? If you have worked through the steps carefully, and practised your coping self-statement, your bad feelings should get less. In our example, Fred might find he now feels only 30 per cent disappointed, which is pretty reasonable under the circumstances.

If Jill reacts constructively to his levelling and request, he may feel even better, both now and in the future. At least he has made it possible for that to happen, which is as much as he can do about changing her behaviour.

In the meantime, he can take two more important steps in making himself feel better. You can think of the steps covered so far as 'fire-fighting'. You do them after you have become aware of feeling very bad, that is, after you must have thought about the situation unrealistically.

In the long run, it would be better not to have the unrealistic thoughts in the first place, and so not to have to try these steps to reduce your exaggerated bad feelings. That's what Steps 5 and 6 are all about: helping you to think straighter in the future and so not suffer from exaggerated bad feelings.

Step 5: Challenge the underlying irrational beliefs If someone made three statements to you, during a conversation, like: 'I wouldn't eat a pineapple if you paid me?', 'Pineapples are messy', and 'Who'd be silly enough to buy a pineapple to eat' you would guess that he had an underlying and obviously negative attitude towards pineapples.

All of our statements, including the ones we make to ourselves, reflect our underlying attitudes and beliefs. If your self-talk in a situation is unrealistic or unreasonable, that's because your attitudes towards such situations are irrational.

To stop yourself from thinking unrealistically in those situations in the future, you need to identify your irrational belief(s) about such situations, and replace them with more rational attitudes. Sounds complicated, but really it's not hard. Here's how.

On pages 123–4 there are ten popular irrational beliefs that an American psychologist, Dr Albert Ellis, has suggested underlie most psychological problems. The idea is that we have all wound up with a common set of Irrational Beliefs as a result of being exposed to similar cultural influences in our homes, schools and society.

We don't all believe the same ideas to the same extent, but it does seem to be the case that we have all been influenced by at least some of these ideas. In this step, you try to find which Irrational Belief most closely matches your original self-talk. Sometimes more than one applies; just note down all of them that seem likely to have contributed to your self-talk.

If you weren't able to identify your self-talk in the first place, just see which Irrational Beliefs seem to fit your situation. With a bit of thought, you can usually work this out.

Once you have identified the Irrational Belief(s) that set you thinking unrealistically in this situation, replace it or them with the corresponding Rational Idea(s) from pages 124–5. The Rational Ideas are, we think, more realistic and rational ways of thinking about these situations. The numbers match: you should, for example, replace Irrational Belief No. 6 with Rational Idea No. 6.

Once you have identified the appropriate Rational Idea(s) for your situation, practise it (or them). Replacing your old, irrational thoughts with new, more rational ones should make a difference in the future. If the situation is one that crops up frequently and has caused you a lot of trouble in the past, it can be helpful to write out the Rational Idea(s) on a small card. Carry the card around with you, and rehearse your new rational thoughts often.

TEN POPULAR IRRATIONAL BELIEFS

1 I must be loved or liked and approved of by every person in my life.

2 I must be completely competent, make no mistakes and achieve all the time if I am to be considered worthwhile.

3 Some people are bad, wicked or evil, and they should be punished for this.

4 It is dreadful, nearly the end of the world, when things aren't how I want them to be.

5 My bad feelings are caused by things outside my control, so I can't do anything about them.

6 If something might be dangerous, unpleasant or frightening, I should worry about it a lot.

7 It's easier to put off something difficult or unpleasant than it is to face up to it.

8 I need to depend on someone stronger than myself.

9 My problem(s) was (were) caused by some event(s) in my past, so that's why I have it (them) now.

10 I should be very upset by other people's problems and difficulties.

TEN RATIONAL IDEAS

1 I want to be loved or liked and approved of by some of the people in my life. I will feel disappointed or lonely when that doesn't happen, but I can cope with those feelings, and I can take constructive steps to make and keep better relationships.

2 I want to do some things well, most of the time. Like everybody, I will occasionally fail or make a mistake. Then I will feel bad, but I can cope with that, and I can take constructive steps to do better next time.

3 It is sad that most of us do some bad things from time to time, and some people do a lot of bad things. But making myself upset won't change that.

4 It is disappointing when things aren't how I would like them to be, but I can cope with that. Usually I can take constructive steps to make things more as I would like them to be but, if I can't, it doesn't help me to exaggerate my disappointment.

5 My problem(s) may be influenced by factors outside my control, but my thoughts and actions also influence my problem(s), and they **are** under my control.

6 Worrying about something that might go wrong won't stop it from happening; it just makes me unhappy now! I can take constructive steps to prepare for possible problems, and that's

as much as anyone can do. So I won't dwell on the future now.

7 Facing difficult situations will make me feel bad at the time, but I can cope with that. Putting off problems doesn't make them any easier, it just gives me longer to worry about them.

8 It's good to get support from others when I want it, but the only person I really **need** to rely on is myself.

9 My problem(s) may have started in some past events, but what keeps it(them) going now is my thoughts and actions, and they are under my control.

10 It is sad to see other people in trouble, but I don't help them by making myself miserable. I can cope with feeling sad, and sometimes I can take constructive steps to help others.

Continuing our example:

> Fred appears to have been influenced here by Irrational Beliefs 1 (he is telling himself he **must** have Jill's affection and approval), 3 (he is telling himself she is a bad person because she is just using him to get money), 4 (he is exaggerating how bad it is that she hasn't asked about his day), and 5 (he is blaming her for his bad feelings).
>
> Fred would now spend a few minutes reading over Rational Ideas 1, 3, 4 and 5, thinking about how they apply to this situation.

Step 6: Reward your successes People are more likely to keep doing things they are rewarded for doing. If you would like to change your self-talk in a rational direction, and keep it that way, you should reward your attempts to do so. So, when you try these steps and cope with troublesome situations better, give yourself a pat on the back.

Concluding our example:

> Finally Fred told himself, 'Hey, I handled that much better! In the past I would have sulked about Jill ignoring my day until we had an argument. Now I feel much better, and she is taking much more interest in my work.'

If a part of your new strategy includes changing your behaviour, and the changes you are aiming for are big, take it one step at a time. People learn by succeeding; failure and mistakes only discourage you. Set realistic goals for change, take them one at a time, and recognise your achievement of each one.

Finally, you should note that you can do the whole of this exercise before an event to help you handle it better. So, if you see a coming situation, in which you expect to feel very bad, go through all of the steps beforehand. Challenge your self-talk about the situation, learn off by heart a coping self-statement to use in the situation, and revise your attitudes towards it by swapping over to more rational ideas about it. Here is an example of this whole process, going on in one relationship:

John had asked Rose a number of times to remember to put the milk in the fridge. (We know this sounds trivial, but so are many of the issues couples fight over.) The milk is out on the kitchen bench and it is a hot day. John walks into the kitchen.

John's feeling when he sees the milk: Annoyed (75 per cent)
John's self-talk: 'Bloody Rose, she never remembers to put the milk away. She never does anything I ask.'
John's behaviour: he shouts, 'Rose, why the hell can't you remember to put the milk away. You never do anything I ask, even simple things!'

Rose's feeling when John shouts at her: Angry and defensive (90 per cent)
Rose's self-talk: 'There he goes again, always shouting at me about the stupidest things. He can never make a civil request!'
Rose's behaviour: she shouts back, 'Why do you always have to scream at me? Put the bloody milk away yourself!'

It's not hard to see where this couple is headed, towards Round 6,904 in the continuing fight that their relationship has become. Both partners are thinking and acting in ways that will escalate the discussion into a full-blown argument.

Since John began that round of overreaction and over-kill, we'll begin by showing how he could have handled the situation better. Let's start the scene again with John walking into the kitchen to find the milk on the bench.

John's initial feelings and thoughts are the same as before, but this time he recognises that feeling so bad is a signal to him to check his own self-talk before he does anything else.

John's further thoughts: 'Hold it! I'm just making myself angry and that will just lead to us having another fight. We need another fight like I need another hole in the head. Now, how realistic am I being? Well, it is bloody annoying when Rose forgets to put away the milk, but she doesn't really do it all the time, and I guess I don't always do what she asks.

'I am annoyed about it, but I'll survive that, and there's no point blowing it up out of proportion. I'll go and level with her about it, and ask her to try to remember to put the milk away on hot days.'

By the end of this review of his self-talk, John had reduced his annoyance to the more reasonable level of 35 per cent and he could cope with this while he made a levelling statement to Rose. Later, when he looked back over his original reaction, he recognised he was buying into Irrational Beliefs 3 (blaming Rose) and 4 (exaggerating how bad the situation was).

He spent a few minutes reading over Rational Ideas 3 and 4, and fitting them to this situation, and to his relationship with Rose in general. Gradually he finds that he is losing his temper less, and is more likely to make a constructive response to events which had previously led to arguments.

In the best of all possible worlds, John would use constructive thoughts and actions like these every time something upsets him. In the real world, from time to time, he'll fall back into his old thinking habits, exaggerate his feelings, and attack Rose again. How could she handle that better?

Rose's initial feelings and thoughts when John shouts at her are the same as before. But she, too, is learning that when she feels really bad that's a signal to check her own self-talk before she does anything else.

Rose's further thoughts: 'Hold it! I do feel angry when John shouts at me, but I don't want any more fights. It's a pity that he is overreacting like this, but I can cope with that, and I'm not going to overreact back. I'll see if I can level with him, and get him to level with me.'

Rose's annoyance subsided to 30 per cent, especially because she saw she was being constructive even though John was shouting at her. She levelled with him about how she felt when he shouted at her, and felt pleased with herself for handling the situation much better.

Later, she recognised that her initial reactions' had been exaggerated by Irrational Beliefs 3 (blaming John) and 4 (wishing he would act differently, but not doing anything about it), so she rehearsed Rational Ideas 3 and 4 and tried to fit them to her situation. She is now finding she can handle John's occasional losses of temper much better.

Most people find it hard to change their automatic thoughts at first. It usually requires some persistence and repeated practice to change over-learned habits. It can help if you do it as a written exercise whenever possible. Even if you can't write out the steps at the time, do it as soon as possible afterwards. Writing makes you slow down and think more carefully.

An Important Rule of Thumb

Only you, as an individual, can check your own self-talk and, when necessary, change it. We made this point in Chapter 3, when we discussed changing your self-talk to help in improving your communication, and we want to emphasise it again here.

Most of the relationship skills described in this manual take two people, because the relationship exists between them. But your self-talk is an individual responsibility, and changing it to be more realistic is an individual contribution each of you makes to the success of the relationship.

By now we hope you understand why it is simply untrue, and therefore self-defeating, to blame your partner for your bad feelings. It is true that your partner influences how you feel, but finally it is your thoughts and actions that determine how you feel, and changing them is your responsibility.

PRACTICAL EXERCISE
Changing your self-talk

Go back to your bad feelings diary and look for a situation that often leads to your feeling bad. Work through the six steps above. Write out an appropriate coping self-statement and the appropriate Rational Idea(s) on a card. Carry the card with you and practise your new self-talk often.

The next time that situation occurs, see how much better you cān handle it by thinking straighter and acting constructively (the next section has some ideas on constructive actions). If you need to, take the card out and refresh your rational thinking during the situation.

Beware of the hidden agenda

Do you often get a *déjà vu* feeling when you fight? Do you find yourselves fighting over the same old topics, saying the same old things, ending in the same old way with nothing really resolved?

Some couples repeatedly argue over the same issues. Sometimes this is because they lack the communication and problem-solving skills to resolve genuine issues. Applying yourselves to Chapters 3, 6 and 7 should change that.

But sometimes it's because the content of the argument is not the real issue. In Chapter 3 we talked about 'hidden agendas', unspoken fears of losing your partner's love, or of losing power in the relationship. Because these fears are what are really causing the argument, but they are not being discussed, not surprisingly the arguments never really get resolved.

If there is a pattern in your relationship of repetitive but fruitless arguments, check your own self-talk again. What do you really want from the argument – to decide who does the dishes next (or whatever trivial issue you are shouting about), or are you really asking your partner to prove she loves you or trying to make him follow orders?

If there is a chance that your arguments stem from these unspoken fears, go back and revise that section in Chapter 3.

SHARED FIGHT CONTROL SKILLS

Tracking troublesome situations and the common triggers of your fights

Some couples seem to choose the worst possible times to try to solve problems. The bedlights have just gone out, both are tired and need to sleep, and a small voice says, 'Dear, there's something I want to say'. No-one is going to find it easy to keep their cool under those circumstances.

We have formed the impression that half the domestic

disputes in Australia are about navigating the family car. Whichever partner is looking at the map is automatically an incompetent clot who couldn't read the alphabet, while the partner driving is invariably too fast and too impatient.

We have found that many couples can predict with some accuracy what they will fight over, when and where. Now we want to suggest you make use of that information.

PRACTICAL EXERCISE

Tracking troublesome situations

Solving problems and resolving conflicts take some time, some concentration and some patience with each other. If you try to raise issues at times when you can't meet these prerequisites, don't be surprised if the discussion becomes an argument.

There is nothing more difficult or frustrating than trying to hold an important conversation with someone who is dashing around getting dressed, or cooking, or looking at television, or dropping off to sleep in bed. These situations increase your feelings of frustration and set you up for an argument.

Record when your arguments typically happen. Is it at a certain time of day (early evening is quite common)? Or in a certain situation (visiting the family, driving in the car, or whatever)? Do they happen a lot just before she gets her period? No, we are not being sexist. Premenstrual tension is a very real phenomenon, and a real problem for some women, and thus for their relationships. If you (the woman in this relationship) find your mood just before your period is causing you unreasonable distress and contributing to arguments in the relationship, your family doctor may be able to offer some helpful advice. In any case, we have found that women can cope better with the hormonal stress of this time by using the steps outlined above for feeling better by thinking straighter. If this applies to you, take the time now to work through those steps and prepare a coping self-statement and some rational ideas for your next period.

When you have identified the common triggers for your arguments, discuss strategies to prevent important discussions occurring at those times. One important step is to work out a time, suitable to both of you, when you can sit down without interruptions and calmly discuss any current issues.

This may sound very organised, and some couples initially don't like the idea. But they soon find a dramatic improvement in their relationship when they discuss issues regularly, and at a time that is suitable for both of them.

This discussion period should not take up large amounts of time. You could set aside 20 minutes, each night or second night, to discuss any important issues that occurred in your relationship within the last day or two. Use your communication skills, and try to discuss both good and bad events, sharing both good and bad feelings.

Structured time like this makes it easier to bring up issues that may have bothered either one of you. In the future you may become more comfortable about asking for a discussion session. But at the moment it may be easier for both of you if time is set aside for discussions.

Don't let these discussion times become bitching sessions and **do** remember to use your communication skills and then problem-solving skills.

You will also need to consider how you can postpone issues until your discussion time. This may mean that you will sometimes feel frustrated for a few hours. That is preferable to trying to have a discussion at an inappropriate time, and then arguing.

Of course, if an issue is genuinely urgent, you may make an exception and stop what you are doing to discuss something on the spot. But generally it is possible to suspend your discussion until a better time later.

PRACTICAL STEPS TO STOP FIGHTS

1 Stop Action

By Stop Action we mean putting yourself in the role of a movie director, watching you and your partner playing the scene in which tempers are rising. As soon as you notice this, that one or both of you is becoming angry, stop the action! Stop the discussion **before** it becomes an argument.

Tracking your arousal becomes important in using Stop Action. If you are unaware of your increasing arousal, then it becomes difficult to use Stop Action effectively, before an argument has developed. It is better to use Stop Action too early than too late. You do not need further practice in arguing. You probably do that quite well. You now need to practise stopping discussions from becoming arguments.

You may find it easier to take this step if you refresh your memory of the myths about arguments in Chapter 1. Arguments are destructive: they destroy the good faith between you and your partner. Even the occasional fight can be destructive. In anger you both may say things you later regret. But it is not possible to go back and not say them – all the apologies in the world do not change what was said.

This is not to say that there won't be times when one of you gets heated during a discussion. But that is all that needs to occur. At that point, you call a Stop Action. You then have two choices: can you pick up the discussion again straight away, but handle it better by using your relationship skills for communication and problem solving?

Or, are you too upset to do this? Is any attempt to talk further just going to lead to an argument? If so, go immediately to the next step.

2 Take Time Out

This means to take Time Out from the discussion so that you can cool down, and then come back and do it better. If necessary, go to different rooms while you cool down.

Time Out can serve two useful functions **if** you use it constructively. Use it to cool down. Then use it to work out how **you** (not your partner) could have dealt more constructively with the situation.

In other words, put as much effort into reviewing the process of your discussion – and what was going wrong with it – as you put into reviewing its content, and what you think was wrong with that. You can very usefully begin by checking your own self-talk.

Either one of you can suggest Time Out. Ideally, the one who is more upset will take this constructive initiative: 'Hold it! I'm starting to get angry. If we go on now, I'll lose my temper and we'll have another stupid fight. I would like Time Out to cool down.'

But if you see your partner is losing control and hasn't called a Time Out, you can take the initiative: 'You are getting angry, and if we go on I'll probably get angry, too. Let's take Time Out.'

3 Make an appointment

Time Out is **not** walking out. Just walking out on your

partner in the middle of a discussion is a very aggressive thing to do. Effectively, you are saying to your partner, 'You aren't worth talking to'. Even if you don't intend it that way, don't be surprised if that's how it seems to your partner.

You avoid that risk, when using Time Out properly, by always making a precise appointment to return to the discussion, before you take Time Out. 'I'm too upset to go on talking about this now; I would like to take half an hour to cool down', or 'I would like to pick up this discussion after the children have gone to bed'.

As well as avoiding the risk of Time Out being seen as aggressive, making an appointment to return to the topic means that neither of you has to take the responsibility for raising the issue again. You have already agreed when you will do that.

4 Later

When you get back together at the appointed time to discuss the issue again, first each of you should check how you are feeling. Are you ready for constructive discussion, or do you need to take more Time Out? It is frustrating to have to keep postponing the resolution of your problem, but that's less distressing for you and your relationship than fighting.

When you both feel calm enough to go on with the discussion, make sure you deliberately use your communication and problem-solving skills. If feelings become heated again, use your fight control skills again. And always watch your own self-talk.

SOME TIPS FOR FIGHT CONTROL

1 Learn to track your own arousal

We believe that both individuals in a relationship are responsible for any argument. No-one can continue an argument alone. It takes two to argue. Learn to track your own level of arousal, and to use it as a signal for checking and changing your own self-talk and actions. You can't improve the relationship single-handed, but you can make an essential individual contribution to fight control.

2 Replay discussions

At a time when you and your partner have cooled down, replay the discussion and try to find out where you went wrong. There is one golden rule for this exercise: focus on what **you** could have changed. **Do not** criticise your partner, no matter how wrong you think she may have been.

Use the procedure we recommended in Chapter 3, of recording these practice discussions to hear how you really sound.

3 Suggesting Time Out

Be careful about how you suggest Time Out.

Do not shout: 'You need Time Out! I won't speak to you for half an hour.'

Do calmly say: 'I am becoming very upset and I suggest we have a Time Out. Could we discuss this issue in two hours?'

Time Out is not a weapon; it should be a constructive step.

4 Recycle fight control skills

Recycle your fight control skills whenever you need them, until you are able to level, listen and validate on that particular topic. Some people initially react to fight control procedures like Stop Action and Time Out by saying, 'Oh, it's so unnatural'.

Why fighting is supposed to be more natural in a love relationship eludes us. In other areas of human activity, it has become a traditional procedure for two warring parties to call a truce in hostilities, so that they can negotiate a mutually acceptable, constructive settlement to their dispute. It seems to be generally accepted that this is better than continuing to shoot at each other.

We don't hear anyone supporting war by saying it's 'natural'. Neither are arguments in relationships. Fight control skills may be new to you, but that doesn't make them 'unnatural'.

5 Discussing difficult issues

If you are going to discuss an issue that you know has been difficult in the past, you should both be careful to check your own self-talk, your own arousal, and your use of communication skills. At first, you can even stop every few sentences and review your progress. This can be a clumsy way of discussing something, but it does help to prevent arguments when you face up to the contentious issues in your relationship, which you must do eventually.

6 Reward yourselves

Give yourselves a pat on the back every time you are successful at using your fight control skills. You may feel bad for a little while after the discussion, but you can tell yourself that you handled the situation better than before.

You could even reward yourselves by doing something nice together.

PRACTICAL EXERCISE
Fight control

It is much easier to practise fight control skills before you get into an argument. Then when your feelings are really getting high, you automatically know what to do.

Agree on a time to discuss a relatively neutral topic, but with the aim of trying out fight control skills.

Discuss the weather, or your job, or the nextdoor neighbours. This will appear strange at first, but it is important you learn the skills **before** you need them.

Practise this a few times. Then use more important issues in your discussion.

You will begin to learn to cope with the frustration of stopping a conversation that is important to you. This is one of the most difficult aspects of fight control, to learn to put off something that feels important.

Arguments serve no useful purpose in your relationship. Take the time now to learn how to prevent them.

6
Solving problems in relationships

All relationships have problems. In fact, distressed and non-distressed couples report much the same problems. What distinguishes between the two groups is how they tackle the problems.

In distressed relationships, the two parties will either avoid facing up to problems, or try to coax or force each other into accepting their respective solutions.

In successful relationships, the two parties can sit down and negotiate solutions that are reasonably acceptable to both. In this chapter we will outline how to do this.

The first step is to decide whether the problem you are experiencing is internal or external to your relationship.

DECIDING WHETHER THE PROBLEM IS INTERNAL OR EXTERNAL TO YOUR RELATIONSHIP

All of us can have living problems which affect our relationship. You may have noticed you sometimes come home feeling bad because you had a difficult time at work, or you feel hassled due to family problems, or you may feel depressed or angry over some part of your life.

None of us can separate one part of our lives from the rest. Feelings that we experience in one area of our lives will be carried with us into our relationships. If this happens too often, it may also become an issue in the relationship, but it is important to distinguish the origin of your bad feelings.

An external problem is one which originates, and can only be solved, outside the relationship. Will asking your partner to change his behaviour solve your problem, or do you really

WIZARD OF ID

need to look at the other areas of your life for the solution to your problem? Do you need to look at reducing your job stress, or changing your feelings of depression, or improving your social skills, or some other solution not directly involving your partner?

Your relationship can offer support and help for both partners when you have outside difficulties. You can discuss your difficulties with each other. You can offer advice to each other, which may be helpful, but at the same time you will have to be prepared to let your partner make her own decision about how she will solve the problem.

If you decide your present problem is an external one, use your communication skills to discuss it with your partner, asking for his advice if necessary.

If your partner wishes to discuss a problem with you, remember also to use your communication skills: listen carefully, validating her feelings and her point of view, offering your help and constructive advice if necessary, but remembering that it will be your partner's decision.

An internal problem is one which originates, and must be solved, within the relationship. Even if you both decide that a problem is primarily external to your relationship, it may still affect your relationship, for example, a job that demands extra time, which means time away from the relationship. You will then need to use the problem-solving skills outlined in the rest of this chapter.

STEPS FOR SOLVING PROBLEMS WITHIN YOUR RELATIONSHIP

1 Have a gripe session

You can begin problem solving in your relationship by first having a gripe session by yourself. This is, write down all the aspects of your relationship that you find disagreeable and would like to change. (Go back to the list you should have done on this topic in the Introduction.)

For example, your list may have items like these:

Dislike coming home from work and having my partner complain about his day. What about me?

Feel resentful for having to take all the responsibility for organising the children. She rarely does anything.

Would like the quality and frequency of our sexual relationship to improve. He doesn't know how to please me.

Want my partner to pay more attention to me. She never pays me any attention; I am like a piece of furniture.

Want my partner to talk about things I am interested in; he is always talking about things I have no interest in.

2 Write positive requests

Initially, while you are griping to yourself, there is no need to be concerned about how you write down your requests for change. We often tend to think in terms of what we do not like, rather than in terms of what we would like. However, it is a very different matter when you present these requests to your partner. Negative or vague requests for change are likely to cause arguments.

The above examples include some requests that are very vague and negative. Before discussing these requests you need to change them to specific, positive requests.

By specific, we mean that you have to define your requests so clearly that there can be no misinterpretation by anyone as to what you are requesting. For example, if you asked your partner to show her love for you more often, you may have had in mind that she initiate sex more often.

But your partner may respond by making you a nice dinner every night, since she thinks this is a good way of 'showing her love' for you. A week later you may complain to your partner that she hasn't done what you asked her to do. She will claim that she has. You have another argument and create more mistrust in your relationship. So you can see why it is very important to be specific and clearly outline your request to your partner.

By positive requests, we mean that you ask your partner to

do something, or more of something, that you would like. If the gripe you start with is something you would like your partner to stop, or do less of, it is up to you to think of the positive alternative which would automatically exclude the behaviour that you don't like.

For example, if you would like your partner to watch less television in the evenings, you would ask him to increase the amount of time he spends in other activities which you like, such as playing cards together. This would automatically cut down on his television-watching.

Or, if you would like your partner to stop coming home late, you would ask her to come home early or on time. This will automatically cut out coming home late.

Focussing on negative gripes revives bad feelings, and can lead to you simply swapping complaints. Focussing on the positive alternative means you are always talking about changes you would like, and this should generate more good feelings. It gets away from the old accusations and into constructive change.

The other advantage to specific, positive requests is that they give your partner much more useful information about what you want. For example, if you said to your partner, 'I don't want to go out on Saturday night', or being even more specific, 'I don't want to go to Charlie's party on Saturday night', you haven't really told her much about what you **do** want.

On the other hand, if you said, 'I would like us to stay home and have a quiet evening together, playing chess and listening to music', then your partner knows exactly what you want. It is still up to your partner whether or not she agrees with your request, but at least she knows exactly what it is you are requesting.

So the next step is to rewrite your requests as specific, positive requests for change.

For example:

I would find it more enjoyable when I come home, if I was able to spend a few minutes by myself to relax, and then we could sit down with a drink and discuss the day.

I would really appreciate it if we were able to work out a fairer arrangement for sharing responsibility for getting the children off to school, organising sitters, helping them with homework, and asking them to perform tasks around the house.

I would like to double the number of times we have sex, to about two or three times per week. I would also like us to continue the sexual enhancement exercises we have begun, at least once a week.

I would like you to remark on my appearance more often, especially when we go out together. I would also like you to speak more frequently to me when we are with friends.

I would like us to find times when we can sit down together and discuss a book or play or film that we have both read or seen.

Check your requests and make sure

   1 They contain 'I' messages, not 'You' messages.

   2 They are specific, not vague, generalised requests.

   3 They are couched in positive terms, not in terms of what you don't want but in terms of what you would like.

3 Break your problems into manageable steps

Often when people start to tackle problems or try to change things in their lives, they are put off by the size or number of the problems that need to be solved. There's so much that it just doesn't seem worthwhile starting. A basic technique in problem solving is to break your big problems down into smaller steps, or sub-problems.

Then, if there are a lot of them, decide on your priorities. Which steps need to be taken first, because later ones will depend on them, or because they are more pressing, or because solving them will make a bigger difference to the relationship? Number your problems in the order in which you would like to tackle them.

In writing out your problems, it is important to distinguish between what really are your problems – the things or changes you want – from possible solutions – how you might get what you want. Confusing your problems with your solutions restricts your problem-solving potential because you may never go any further than the first solution that came to your mind, and this often isn't the best solution.

Within your relationship, it will be important that the solution you finally choose is one you both accept. You can best achieve this mutual agreement if you have both had a chance to suggest, and then consider, a number of possible solutions.

So now you should revise your list again, with two aims. Break down any big problems into sub-problems or steps. And separate out the problems (what you want) from possible solutions (how you might get it). Use these possible solutions to begin your list of possible solutions, which you will expand later.

Problems	Solutions
I would like to be able to relax when I come home from work.	I could spend a few minutes by myself before we talk together over a drink.
I would like us to share the tasks of:	
1 getting the children off to school	
2 organising sitters	
3 helping children with homework	
4 asking the children to help around the house	
I would like to double the number of times we have sex.	Two or three times per week.
I would like to enhance our sexual relationship.	Continue sexual enhancement exercises.
I would like you to remark on my appearance more often.	
I would like you to speak to me more often when we are with friends.	
I would like us to develop common topics for discussion.	We could read books, see films or plays and discuss them.

When you become more experienced at defining problems clearly, being specific and positive about requests, dividing big problems into manageable steps, and recognising the difference between the problem and your suggested solutions, you will not need to go through these steps so laboriously. For now, we advise you to continue using the above steps by yourself, until you have mastered these aspects of problem solving.

You are then ready to present your problems to each other in an agenda session.

4 Have an agenda session

You have now both aired your gripes to yourselves, and then transformed these gripes into responsible requests for change. The next step is to meet in an agenda session. The idea of an agenda session is to inform your partner of the problems you are having in the relationship.

You need to set aside time, no more than half an hour, when you will be able to sit down together without interruptions. Then present your refined list of problems to each other. You will not be able immediately to resolve all the gripes you have brought up so you will need to decide what gripes will be dealt with first. This is the aim of the agenda session: to present gripes and to decide which ones to work on first.

You have already decided which of your problems are most important to you. Now put your priorities together, and decide which issues you agree to tackle first. If agreement on this isn't easy, you can decide to start with the number one problem of each list.

Remember to use your communication skills during this exercise. You will both have issues that are important to you. This need not cause disagreements if you are prepared to recognise each other's feelings and validate each other's point of view. If there are a large number of issues important for both of you, you may just have to spend more time problem solving.

After you have written out your joint list, starting with the most important issues, arrange times when you will be able to sit down to discuss the first of these. Do not attempt to discuss more than one problem in a problem-solving session.

We recommend that you spend no more than half an hour on each problem-solving session. If the problem has not been dealt with in that time, you should arrange another time to finish your discussion. Remaining cool-headed, calm and fresh is more important when problem solving, especially on the hot issues in your relationship, than trying to solve everything in a day.

In summary, this is all you should do in your agenda session:

1 Show your positive requests to each other.
2 Make a joint list of positive requests, in an agreed order of priority.
3 Make half-hour appointments to begin discussing the problems.
4 Do not plan to discuss more than one problem per session.

Do not go on and immediately attempt to solve problems. Take a break and congratulate yourselves for sorting the issues out this far. Your first problem-solving session should be clearly separated from your agenda session. You have had some of these problems for years, so waiting a few more days to solve them will not harm your relationship.

5 Check your self-talk

We suggest that before you meet together to discuss a certain problem, you both think about the problem individually and begin to do some constructive work. This does not mean to go away to practise bad feelings about the problem. What you can begin to do is think about the changes you could make to help resolve the problem.

Your self-talk, especially any unrealistic expectations, may be part of the problem and you will need to look at these for yourself.

Example
Problem: I would like my partner to take more notice of my appearance.
Self-talk: 'He never notices how I look. He just ignores me, and treats me like a bit of dirt. That lousy so-and-so, when we discuss this I'll make my feelings known and he will have to change.'

This kind of self-talk is most likely to result in anger and resentment, hindering any attempt at problem solving.

Example

Helpful self-talk:'I feel disappointed and hurt that my partner does not pay as much attention to my appearance as I would like but I can cope with these feelings. I am glad we are going to discuss the problem, so we can do something about it.'

This constructive self-talk is more likely to result in your being able to level when appropriate, which will help you stay calm during the problem solving.

Another example

Problem: I would like to discuss finances regularly so that we can work out a budget each month.

Unhelpful self-talk: 'She never tells me what she does with money and then expects me to balance all the accounts. Well, I am fed up with this happening. She will just have to change.'

This self-talk is also likely to lead to anger, and to an argument.

Helpful self-talk: 'I feel angry that my partner spends money which upsets our budget but I can handle this feeling. We have shared our feelings about this issue and now we can try to solve the problem. It may be difficult for both of us to change, but that is better than continuing to bicker about money.'

This self-talk will help you feel able to discuss the issue calmly and reach a satisfactory solution.

You can usefully spend some time between problem-solving sessions analysing your self-talk. Do you have self-talk that is unhelpful and destructive? That is, self-talk that only leads to you feeling bad and then reacting in a way that upsets your partner, and prevents both of you from resolving the problem.

We have previously discussed how to change your self-talk in other relationship skills. If necessary, refer to Chapter 5.

Changing your self-talk is a necessary part of changing feelings and behaviour to improve your relationship. A large part of the distress in relationships is due to the unrealistic and unreasonable self-talk both partners use. The examples of unhelpful self-talk in this manual are typical of the destructive and unnecessary self-talk we have found people use in distressed relationships.

Sometimes unhelpful self-talk can be due to unrealistic expectations.

Example

Unrealistic expectation:	'I want my partner to spend every minute of the day thinking about me and when we are together to pay total attention to me.'
Resulting unhelpful self-talk:	'She never spends enough time with me, or pays me any attention.'
Resulting behaviour:	Over-demanding and excessive jealousy of any of your partner's activities which do not involve you.

In contrast

Realistic expectations:	'It is important for me and my partner to spend time together, but it is also important for both of us to be involved in independent activities.' 'It is important to me to receive compliments from my partner but it is unrealistic to expect my partner always to compliment me. I need to rely on my own self-compliments, which enable me to be independent of other people's praise.'
Resulting helpful self-talk:	'I feel hurt that we do not spend as much time together as I would like. However I can cope with that. I should schedule this for one of our problem-solving sessions.' 'It might be nice to receive compliments from my partner continually but this is unrealistic. It is important that I get this request into proportion. My partner does sometimes compliment me, and I could ask him to do this more frequently.'

Resulting behaviour: More able to cope with your feelings, to recognise your own unrealistic expectations, and to request change in a nondestructive way.

The myths of love and marriage we discussed in Chapter 1 are the basis of most of the unrealistic expectations people bring to their relationships. In the above example, the unrealistic expectations are a product of Myths 1, 9 and 10. You may like to go back to Chapter 1 and refresh your memory of the myths, so that you can be sensitive to their influence in your relationship.

Remember you will not always recognise that you are being influenced by a myth because, when you see it written, it looks so silly. Few people own up to having such unrealistic expectations, yet many people **act** as though they believed the myths.

Look at your **actions** to help you discover whether your expectations are unrealistic. Do not be surprised if you find that you are behaving as though you believe some of the myths. If you are exposed to a set of ideas for years, with little contrary information, some of those ideas are bound to rub off on you.

In Chapter 1 we suggested that you write out your realistic expectations of a better relationship. Revise that list, and perhaps extend it now that you are further into working on your relationship. If your self-talk is making it difficult for you to be constructive in approaching the problems in your relationship, go back and work carefully through the steps in Chapter 5 on how to change your self-talk.

Now you can begin your first problem-solving session.

6 Brainstorm solutions

Write out the first problem you have agreed to solve, on a large piece of paper. Then you brainstorm solutions together. Brainstorming means both of you trying to think up as many solutions to the problem as you can. The golden rule of brainstorming is quantity, not quality.

The idea behind brainstorming is to free up your creativity, so that you have your best chance of coming up with the best solution, which may be quite different from what you first had in mind.

There are a few rules that you need to follow to get the most out of your brainstorming. The aim is to think up as many solutions as possible. Do not criticise any solutions yet. You should not criticise or evaluate your partner's solutions. Just write them down.

Say everything that comes into your head. Do not prevent yourself from suggesting something. Even if the suggestion is a silly one, say it. Silly suggestions add fun to your brainstorming session, and may lead to good ideas.

Let's take one of our previous examples:

Problem: Equal responsibility for getting the children off to school.
Brainstorming: We could be responsible for one child each in the morning.
               We could take turns every other morning.
               We could encourage the children to get themselves off to school.
               We could employ someone to get the children off to school.
               We could ask the older child to be responsible for himself and we can take turns with the younger.
               The older child could look after himself and his brother in the morning.

Another example of brainstorming:

Problem: I would like you to notice my appearance more often.
Brainstorming: Every second morning you could pay me a compliment.
               I could mention your appearance when we go out.
               You could wear your red dress more often; red suits you.
               I could pay more attention to my appearance, particularly when we go out.
               You could remind me to notice you.
               I could pin a sign inside your wardrobe, 'Remember to comment on Jan's appearance.'
               You could pin a sign on yourself, 'Please notice me.'

I could ask you what you thought of my appearance.
You could occasionally buy a new dress and get your hair done.
I could buy some nice perfume and wear it more often.
I could buy a sexy outfit to wear around the house when we have a date at home.

7 Weigh up the pros and cons of each solution

After you have brainstormed your list of suggestions and cannot think of any more, weigh up the pros and cons of each solution.

We usually suggest that couples do this individually at first. Each take a copy of the suggested solutions and write next to each solution what you see as its advantages and disadvantages. Also put a ' + ' next to any solution you would be willing to try, and a ' − ' next to any solution you would not be willing to try.

Then rank the + solutions in order of their appeal to you, 1 for the solution you would most prefer, 2 for the next, and so on. If you can't see much difference between some solutions, you can give them the same number.

Each partner's ratings may look like this:

Jan's ratings:
1 You could mention my appearance when we go out.
1 I could pay more attention to my appearance, particularly when we go out. +
1 I could wear my red dress more often. +
2 I could buy a sexy outfit to wear around the house on our dates at home. +
3 I could buy perfume and wear it. +
3 I could occasionally buy a new dress and get my hair done. +
4 I could pin a note in your wardrobe. +
5 I could remind you to comment on my appearance. +
6 I could pin a sign on myself. −
7 Every second morning you could comment on my appearance. −

Arthur's ratings looked like this:

1 You could pay more attention to your appearance particularly when we go out. +
1 You could buy a sexy outfit. +
1 You could buy nice perfume. +
2 I could comment on your appearance when we go out. +
2 You could occasionally buy yourself a new dress and get your hair done. +
2 You could wear your red dress more often. +
3 Every second morning I could pay you a compliment. +
4 You could remind me to notice your appearance. +
5 You could pin a note inside my wardrobe. −
5 You could pin a note on yourself. −

For the moment forget any solutions that you have both rated as solutions you would least like to try, or not be willing to try at all.

The couple above could agree to discard solutions 3, 4 and 5 for him and 4, 5, 6 and 7 for her.

Now use your communication skills to discuss the remaining solutions one at a time.

This is how Arthur and Jan's discussion went:

Jan: 'If you would notice my appearance, particularly when we go out, I would feel more desirable.'

Arthur: 'You said, if I notice your appearance, particularly when we are going out, you feel desirable. I find it easier to notice and comment on your appearance when you dress up, for instance when we go out with friends. I would like you to dress like that when you go out with me. You can look very attractive when you pay attention to your appearance and I feel good when I am with you.'

Jan: 'You said that I look attractive when I get dressed up and you feel good, although you would like me to do this more often when we are alone. I guess I do dress up more when we are going out with other people. I'm willing to change this. The rest of our solutions indicate some of the things I could do. At the same time I would appreciate help from you. If you could comment on my appearance, I would feel more attractive and inclined to pay attention to my appearance.'

The couple in the above example are able non-defensively to work out a solution that suits both of them. You can see that it is just as important to use communication skills during negotiations as it is in earlier stages when you were discussing the problem.

8 Select a solution to try

Jan and Arthur are beginning to reach a point in their discussion where they will be ready to try a solution. Their final solution will probably be a combination of a number of their suggested solutions.

What have you and your partner decided to try? Are you both willing to try one solution? If so, how are you going to make sure the change occurs? If either of you has requested behaviour changes of the other as a part of your solution, you will need the skills in the next chapter.

This can be a difficult discrimination to make, because almost every problem solution involves some change in behaviour. The point is really whether it was some aspect of your partner's behaviour that created a problem for you in the first place, and so changing his behaviour has always been your goal in this situation.

For example, you may have begun this exercise by wishing your partner would watch less television and spend more evening time interacting with you. This necessarily means you are going to ask her to change some part of her behaviour, and for that you will need the skills in the next chapter.

On the other hand, the problem may not have begun with your dissatisfaction about your partner's behaviour, but something from outside the relationship. For example, one of you may be offered a new job interstate. If he takes it, it means higher salary and better opportunities for promotion, but it also means leaving behind friends, children changing schools, and so on.

The focus of solving this sort of problem is not changing each other's behaviour, but working out a solution that best suits all involved. If you are working on this kind of problem, you can go straight ahead with the steps below.

In our example, Jan and Arthur have both decided that they need to change certain behaviours. Old behaviours, especially old habits, are not easy to change. You may require some help and this is what we discuss in the next chapter.

When you have decided on the solution you will try, you should go ahead and plan exactly how it will be carried out. Who is going to organise the change? What practical steps do you have to take? Do you need any resources? Who will do what, and by when?

9 Try out your solution

Follow your plan through, one step at a time. If it works, great! You have solved one of the problems in your relationship and, possibly more important, you have shown yourselves that you can do this through an essentially co-operative exercise.

If it doesn't work, that's disappointing, but don't get it out of proportion (revise the straight-thinking principles in Chapter 5 if necessary). Give yourselves permission to feel disappointed, but use the 'failure' as a learning opportunity.

Why didn't your solution work? What new information does that give you about the problem? Do you need to brainstorm some more solutions, or is one of your previous ideas now more suitable? Recycle the problem-solving process until you have a successful solution, or you have clearly established that this is a problem you cannot solve within your relationship.

10 Recycle problem-solving skills

Do not try to push your partner into trying a solution she is not happy with.

Problem solving, as we said earlier, should arrive at a win-win situation, where all parties are happy with the outcome. If you are reaching a stalemate, you need to recycle the problem-solving process. This can be a bit frustrating, if you reach this point and aren't able to agree on a solution.

But it is better to find out now that one or both of you is not happy with the solution than to go away, either feeling that the problem has been resolved or that you are reluctantly giving in to a solution that does not suit you. If you leave problem solving with these feelings, you set yourselves up for difficulty in the future. No one really accepts changing in a way that they do not like, no matter what they may initially think they can do.

If you have to recycle the problem-solving process, leave it for another time. You will both probably be tired by this stage, so it is not advisable that you continue. Make another appointment to discuss the problem again. When you return to discuss the problem, go back to the beginning of the process and work through again.

Have you defined the problem accurately? Sometimes couples we see in therapy start with what they think is the problem but after trying to solve the problem realise that another issue was involved which was more important.

Have you been specific enough when defining the problem? If the problem is too broad, you can often get into difficulty when trying to solve it.

Have you brainstormed enough solutions? Do you need to go back and think of other ways of solving the problem?

Have you discarded a solution that may have been worth trying? Go back over the solutions, weighing up the pros and cons again.

Have you checked your self-talk? If you have unhelpful self-talk, such as, 'We will never solve this, we can't agree on anything', then you are unlikely to feel in a suitable frame of mind to solve problems. Instead, try more helpful self-talk, such as, 'We are having difficulty coming to an agreement over this, but it is important that both of us are happy with the solution. It is frustrating to have to go through the process again but that is better than prematurely agreeing to something one or both of us won't be happy with in the future.' Or, you may need to be saying to yourself, 'I feel disappointed that we have not reached a solution, but I can handle that. It is important that we find a solution that suits both of us.'

Let's look at a problem-solving session that ended in a stalemate, and then at how the couple resolved this situation.

Isabel and Fred had been attempting to problem solve on the issue of independent recreational activities. Fred had become involved in a number of sporting organisations and was spending time away from home four nights a week and one day of the weekend. Isabel was often at home, and tended to rely on Fred for adult companionship.

Their agenda session:

 Isabel requested that Fred stay home more often.

 Fred requested that Isabel become involved in more independent activities so that she could develop more adult relationships.

Their brainstorming solutions:

Isabel's suggestions were: Fred go out one night a week.

 Fred stay home at the weekend.

 Fred give up some of his sporting activities.

Fred's suggestions were: Fred mind the kids one night a week so that Isabel could go out.

 Isabel join a local jazz ballet class.

 Isabel join Fred one night a week at the football club.

 Isabel go to cooking classes during the day.

 Isabel take up a hobby during the day.

 Isabel play tennis on Saturday while Fred is at the football.

 Fred and Isabel take the children to the football on Saturday.

Their weighing up of pros and cons:

 Fred and Isabel could not agree on any of these suggestions. Fred preferred all the solutions that involved Isabel doing something for herself without him. Isabel preferred the solutions that involved Fred giving up some of his recreational time. They were reaching a stalemate in their problem solving.

 Recycling problem solving:

 Calmly Fred and Isabel went over each step of their problem solving. They decided that their brainstorming solution could be combined to make a solution more satisfactory for both of them.

 After some negotiation they came up with:

 Fred to go out one night a week; Isabel to go out another night a week; they would both go to Fred's football night, which Isabel enjoyed. They would spend Saturday engaged in independent activities, Fred at the football, taking the children with him, while Isabel played tennis. A further solution they were going to try was for Isabel to find a part-time job. Fred was going to help her do this with the contacts he had at work.

Now begin your problem solving. Start with easier problems, as this enables you to grasp the problem-solving process before you start on more difficult problems where feelings may distract you.

We have found that many couples benefit from having a practice run, on a non-issue, which allows them to concentrate on mastering the skills, before they try them out on the real issues in their relationship. If you think this would help you, try the following.

PRACTICAL EXERCISE

Trial problem solving

Samantha and John always had disagreements over who would put the garbage bin out. How will they solve this?
One of you can be Samantha, and the other John. Write out your responses to the steps below.
Agenda session
Samantha: 'I would like you to increase. . .'
John: 'I would like you to increase. . .'
Brainstorm solutions
Weigh up pros and cons
Samantha's solutions   John's solutions

Select a solution to try. Discuss how to implement this solution.

Now try this example.
How will Barbara and Laurence solve the problem of how to handle the children when they are disobedient?
Go through the steps together, as with the previous example, but this time swap roles. If you played Samantha last time, now take on the role of Laurence; if you played John last time, now play Barbara.

Are you experiencing any difficulties with these examples? If so, go back and read the instructions again. If you are having difficulty with these trial runs, it will be even harder when you try to solve your own problems, so make sure everything is clear before you start on your problem solving.

The final step in problem solving is to review the **process** rather than the **content**. How does it **feel** for each of you? If problem solving is working, it should lead to feelings of co-operation and increased commitment and faith in the relationship. If this isn't happening, is that because you are not following the steps fully? Or because of unhelpful self-talk?

BUT WE COULD NEVER AGREE

That's possible. Problem solving is a procedure that gives you your best chance of finding a solution to your problems, but it does not guarantee that you will find a solution that reasonably suits you both. Sometimes no amount of brainstorming can discover a mutually acceptable solution because you each want or expect things so completely different.

If you finally decide that a problem in your relationship is insoluble, you then each have to decide how important that is to you. Is this a central and recurring issue? Will this difference keep causing arguments and strife?

If it's big enough, an insoluble difference could be a sensible reason for quitting the relationship (see Chapter 10). On the other hand, you may decide that, on balance, it isn't that important. Yes, this problem bugs you, but there is so much else right about the relationship that you can accept this difference.

It's much easier to do this if the rest of the relationship is genuinely rewarding (see Chapters 1 and 4). So you may want to be certain that you have tried reasonably hard to establish this, before you decide that an insoluble problem is important enough to quit the relationship.

7
Changing how you behave

HOW YOU INFLUENCE YOUR PARTNER'S BEHAVIOUR, OR WHO GOES FIRST?

Have you noticed that the way you behave influences other people's behaviour? People 'train' each other to react in certain ways. We are all influenced, throughout our lives, by other people. Just as you influence your children, you also influence other adults, although many people do not recognise that this is what they are doing.

Have you ever said something or done something, and had the person you were with react badly? Did this make you more cautious about repeating that behaviour in front of that person? That person has influenced your behaviour.

Even in those cases when you don't like the other person, or are unconcerned by his response, and you continue to behave in that way in front of him, he has still influenced your behaviour. Your disregard for him has led you to choose to continue to behave in that way in front of him.

Recent psychological research has shown that people are able to change throughout their whole lives. People do not develop a fixed personality some time before they reach adolescence, and stay that way for the rest of their lives. They are much more flexible than this old notion suggested. People can behave differently in different situations. And they can change their behaviour at any time of life.

So what does this mean in the context of your relationship? It means that you, through your behaviour, will be playing a role in how your partner is behaving. The first step to changing your partner's behaviour, and maintaining that change, may be to look at what you are doing.

Example
Judy felt annoyed because her husband, Mike, didn't help around the house. Every time she went to clean up she became angry. She slammed doors and cupboards, crashing objects and moving around in a 'super-efficient' way. Halfway through this performance, Mike would notice and ask if he could help. Judy would immediately snap, 'I don't need any help, thank you'. Mike retired out of her way.

Sometimes Mike would begin to clean up and Judy would immediately nag him to do it the way she wanted things done. Mike would get fed up and leave it.

Mike could not win. When he did help he was told off. When he didn't help he was told off.

Judy could have changed this situation by trying to respond positively to Mike's attempts to help around the house. Eventually Mike would begin to feel good about helping, and be prepared to help more often.

In this example, even if Mike and Judy agreed that Mike needed to help more around the house, if Judy still nagged him when he tried Mike would be unlikely to keep helping.

Example
Every time Amanda did something nice for Stewart he became uneasy. He responded by thanking her gruffly but immediately turning away. Amanda slowly became concerned about his response and so tended to avoid doing nice things for him.

Stewart noticed that Amanda stopped doing these nice things. Even though he had felt uncomfortable, he had enjoyed her thoughtfulness. Now Stewart interpreted her stopping as a sign that Amanda did not care for him as much. He tended to become moody when he was with her.

Amanda responded by also becoming moody and unsure about Stewart's feelings towards her.

You can see how Amanda and Stewart were both influencing each other's behaviour into a negative spiral. Things were getting worse and worse.

We see many couples who have developed these negative spirals in their relationships. Both partners, usually unintentionally, are behaving in ways that increase the negativeness of their interactions. Often both will blame the other; each can see what the other does that is wrong, without realising how much they themselves contribute to the interaction.

Let's look at how Amanda and Stewart could have prevented this from happening:

Possibility 1. Amanda could level to Stewart about how she felt about his turning away when she did something nice. She could also encourage him to respond more positively, by asking him if he liked what she did each time.

Possibility 2. Stewart could level to Amanda about how he liked it when she did something nice, although he found it awkward to accept this. He could also look at his own self-talk leading to this awkward feeling, and take systematic steps to change it (see Chapter 5).

The point is that both partners were contributing to the negative spiral in their relationship, by acting in ways which influenced the other partner to respond negatively. Equally, either partner could break that spiral by using constructive relationship skills to change their own behaviour, and thus their influence on each other.

ANOTHER RULE OF THUMB

You do not effectively get anyone to change their behaviour in ways you would like by nagging, getting upset or yelling. If you nag long enough or yell loudly enough, your partner may grudgingly do what you want, this time. Next time you will have to nag longer or yell more loudly before he does it again. A great deal of research has shown that punishment – verbal, physical, emotional – is an unreliable and messy way of changing behaviour.

Humans basically work for rewards. The rewards may be subtle, or entirely personal and thus initially invisible, but they are there. Some people feel uncomfortable with this view of human motivation, preferring to believe that humans can be moved by 'higher' motives than reward, conveniently ignoring how good it feels to be so noble.

You can pretend there is no law of gravity and step off a cliff, refusing to believe you will fall. As you plummet down, you may have second thoughts. You can pretend there are no laws of human behaviour, and refuse to use anything so 'mechanical' as rewards. As your relationship plummets down, you may have second thoughts.

We have found a little kindness works wonders. People change when they are rewarded for changing. Go back to our exercise of catching your partner doing something nice. Just as negative behaviours can become a vicious cycle, so too positive behaviours can become positive cycles.

If you respond negatively when your partner does something nice for you, don't be surprised if she stops doing nice things. If you nag your partner to try to get him to do what you want, don't be surprised if he does it less. If you respond positively to the nice things your partner does, and you give her encouragement when she tries to change, your relationship has a good chance of becoming more rewarding for both of you.

PRACTICAL EXERCISE

The Magic Pudding Fairy Tale

Read the Magic Pudding Fairy Tale on page 177 together. Then discuss it. What does it mean to you, and your relationship?

A WORD OF WARNING

Negative cycles of behaviour are very destructive to the trust and good faith in relationships. Over time, both partners begin to feel that the other doesn't really care for them. This increases the negativeness of the couple's interactions and their relationship becomes increasingly distressed.

Because of the resulting lack of faith in the relationship, both partners feel less and less inclined to change. They are increasingly less willing to put in the time, effort and risks required to change a relationship. We have found that it is not impossible to change even very distressed relationships, but this depends on both partners being willing to change.

Sometimes the negative exchanges in a relationship have become so frequent and so marked that neither partner is prepared to take the first step in changing, even though both will agree that things need to change. Neither partner is willing to risk feeling vulnerable to the other.

This situation is what we described earlier as a 'stand-off', marked by the 'you-ortas'. Each will suggest that the solution to the relationship's problems is for the other partner to change his behaviour. What this means is that each does not acknowledge the role she plays in influencing the other's behaviour.

If you think your relationship is caught in a stand-off, don't despair. We are not saying that it is necessarily doomed. We are saying that each of you, as individuals, will have to accept some of the responsibility for the negative cycles occurring in your relationship, and be willing to change some of your thoughts and actions to break the cycle.

You must be willing to look, as honestly as possible, at how you contribute to what is going wrong, and decide what you can do to change this. Sometimes this may involve your changing in some ways that you don't really like in themselves, but that are necessary if the relationship is to improve.

This can be uncomfortable (see Chapter 5 for how to cope with that), but you may as well face the fact that you have only two choices: refuse to be the first to change, continue to blame your partner and watch your relationship continue to decline, or grit your teeth and take the first, risky steps yourself. At least in the latter way you have a chance of things improving.

WHAT DO WE CHANGE?

Of course, you have been changing many parts of your relationship already. By now, you should be communicating differently, sharing more pleasure, and so on. As we said in the last chapter, here we want to focus on how to change your behaviour within the relationship where the behaviour itself has become a problem.

At the beginning of this manual we asked each of you to begin a wish list, a list of things you wish would change in the relationship. Now go back and review your wish list. Are there any new items you would like to add, or are there any items on your list that you have already solved or that no longer seem important?

Many couples find it hard to pinpoint what they do or do not like about their relationships, particularly if the relationship has been distressed. The lack of relationship skills that contributed to the distress also makes it hard to recognise why the relationship is distressed.

Improving your communication, coupling, problem solving and other relationship skills may solve some issues, or help you to get others into perspective as unimportant. Fine! **But** we discourage you from skipping this chapter.

The good feelings produced by some constructive changes in a relationship can produce a 'honeymoon' effect. 'Isn't this so much better than before, dear.' Indeed it is, but that doesn't mean there isn't room for further improvement. Honeymoons don't last forever, and unresolved or new problems may eventually need these skills.

It can be easier to tackle some of these remaining issues while you are feeling better about the relationship than it will be if you wait for them to eat up the improvement. So revise your wish list, and see if you can decide exactly what you would now like to change.

For example, your list may look something like this:

'I feel bored when we go out together.'

'I feel unappreciated when we are by ourselves or with other people.'

'I am fed up with always being the one to initiate cleaning the house and making arrangements for the kids.

These are a good start since they identify problems in the relationship for you. But now you need to go through the refining process we described in the last chapter. First, try to be more specific about what is wrong. For example:

'I feel bored when we go out.' Why? Is it because of where we go? No, that's usually interesting. Is it because we see too much of each other? No, if anything we don't see each other enough, at least without distractions. What does happen when we go out? Of course, the conversation always tends to focus on my partner. She never asks how I spent my day or what I have done. She is always talking about herself. Yes, that's it.

'I feel unappreciated when we go out.' Why? Is it because my partner never seems appreciative? No, he does talk with enthusiasm, but only to others, not to me. In fact, he hardly ever talks to me when we are in a group. When we are by ourselves he doesn't seem to have much to say at all. We rarely discuss the news, or current issues, or even our friends.

'I am fed up with always being the one to initiate cleaning the house and arrangements for the kids.' Why? Is she lazy? No, that's silly, she often works quite hard. The problem seems to be that we have different standards: I like the house cleaner and tidier than she does, so I usually push for some cleaning. I guess I also worry more than she does about what will happen to the kids. It's our differences in these expectations that are the problem.

We hope you are beginning to see how important it is to think through issues for yourself first before you turn them into requests for change in your partner. Sometimes you will get a very different view of what is really the problem.

In the first example above, it would have been easy for the partner raising this problem to jump to the conclusion that all they needed was more variety in their outings, and make this request to his partner. This would be unlikely to change the way in which his partner was monopolising the conversation, and the problem would be still there, all the more frustrating.

You will remember from the last chapter that, in addition to making your requests for change specific, you must always make them positive. Although you may begin by thinking of something you would like your partner to stop doing, or do less of, it is up to you to turn this into a request for your partner to do something, or more of something, that will automatically cut out the behaviour you don't like.

Continuing our examples from above:

'When we go out to dinner, I would like you to spend time in our conversation asking me questions about what I did that day, how I am feeling, and so on. I would also like you to start conversations with me about the news, current affairs, other people, and so on.'

'When we go out with other people, I would like you to include me in the conversation by asking my opinion on whatever is being discussed. I would also like you to look at me sometimes, when you are talking to the group.'

'I would like us to draw up an agreement on what household jobs need to be done, when they should be done, and who is going to do them. I would also like us to draw up a similar agreement for the regular tasks of looking after the children.'

Some people feel uncomfortable making such specific requests of their partners. 'After all, if he loved me, he would know what to do, wouldn't he?' 'Isn't this all rather artificial and mechanical?' 'She's only doing it because I asked her, not because she loves me.'

As we said before, your self-talk, including your interpretations of your partner's behaviour, is **your** responsibility. If you prefer to make vague requests to your partner like 'I wish you would show me more respect', or no requests at all because you believe the myth that good relationships occur 'naturally', don't be surprised if you are disappointed.

How would your partner know what to do that would lead to your feeling more respected by him? How would he even know this was worrying you, if you make no requests at all? Of course, it's very pleasant when your partner spontaneously does something that makes you feel good. But that doesn't mean there isn't also room for her to make you feel good in ways requested by you.

PRACTICAL EXERCISE

Writing specific, positive requests

Change the following vague and negative gripes into specific requests for positive change. Do this exercise together, and discuss it as you go.

Negative or vague	Specific and Positive
'You are lazy' becomes	'I would like you to help with the house cleaning.'

Now do the rest yourselves.
'You're immature.'
'You're too soft with the kids.'
'You're a show-off.'
'You never listen.'
'You're always jealous.'

'You don't care how I feel.'
'You don't want me sexually.'
Now take your own gripes, and write them into specific and positive requests.

NEGOTIATING ACCEPTABLE REQUESTS

As we said earlier, there is no guarantee that your partner will necessarily agree to your requests. Framing them as specific and positive requests for change gives him something concrete to react to, but sometimes that reaction will be 'No!'

Example How not to negotiate behaviour change:
Greg had requested that Julie initiate sex at least twice a week. Their conversation went like this:
Julie: 'There's no way I am going to initiate sex. Whenever I have in the past, you just knock me back. Why should I?'
Greg: 'You're my wife, aren't you. Isn't that why we got married? I am fed up with always having to ask for it. I sometimes wonder if you even care about me. You're probably having an affair.'
Julie: 'Me having an affair! You're the sex maniac who ogles at every passing thing in a skirt.'
Greg: 'What about you last week at Mary's party? Spending all night talking to that casanova, Allan.'
Julie: 'At least he's polite and treats me like a woman, which is more than I can say for you. The only time you show any interest in me is when you feel randy.'

STOP!
By now, you should recognise the mistakes this couple are making.
Let's turn the clock back and see how Julie and Greg could have handled this situation in a more productive way.

Example How to negotiate behaviour changes:
Julie: 'I agree that you mostly initiate sex. I can understand that you would like me to show more interest by initiating sex more.'
Greg: 'Yes, well, that is a change I would like you to make.'
Julie: 'I'm not sure that I would be able to initiate sex twice a week. I feel uncomfortable asking you for sex. I could try, but at first I would like to start with once a week.'

Greg: 'I'm disappointed that you only want to initiate sex once a week. Is there something about our relationship that makes you feel uncomfortable about sex?'

Julie: 'I think I'm not sure you really want to have sex with me. You always have your eyes closed, and we hardly kiss anymore.'

Greg: 'So, would you initiate sex more often if we kissed more, and I looked at you more?'

Julie: 'Yes, that's more like our love-making used to be.'

Greg: 'OK. I like kissing and looking at you. I guess our sex life has been in a bit of a rut.'

Julie: 'OK. I'll try to initiate sex at least once a week.'

In this case, the couple were able to agree on behaviour changes.

Unlike the above example, you may disagree with your partner's suggestion. If this is the case, you will need to use your problem-solving skills to resolve the difference of opinion.

Example How not to negotiate behaviour change:
Shirley's gripe was that she was fed up with living in a half finished house. Keith was building the house and had 'promised' to finish it.

Shirley: 'You're a lazy, no good slob. You spend all your time and effort on other people's houses, not on your own.'

Keith: 'Hang on. What are you talking about? You never appreciate what I do. You're always doing that.'

STOP! We hardly have to go any further. Shirley and Keith are unlikely to solve their problems carrying on in that manner.

Here's a more helpful approach.

Example
Shirley first turned her gripe into a positive request: 'I would like you to finish the house.'

Keith: 'I can understand that. I know you don't like living in a half-finished house. The trouble is I have so much work to do that our house has to come last.'

Shirley: 'It is important to me.'

Keith: 'I see the situation like this. We either don't have all the jobs completed around the house, or I do not earn the money I have been earning.'

Shirley: 'Yes, I know. I appreciate you doing extra work. We need the money. Can we try and approach this situation in a different way?'

Keith: 'Let's have a problem-solving session.'

So they move into problem solving:

Problem: How are we going to finish the jobs that need to be done around the house, and still earn as much money as we need.

Brainstorm: Shirley could do some of the work.
They could get someone else in to do the work.
Keith could earn less money and finish the house.
Shirley could lower her expectations for the house.
Shirley and Keith could work on the house.
Shirley could help Keith with his work.

Pros and cons: Shirley and Keith evaluated each solution, writing down the advantages and disadvantages each could see with each suggested solution, giving each solution a + or − rating, and finally ranking them in order of acceptability.

Solution: Shirley and Keith decided to combine several of their suggested solutions, so that Shirley would make positive comments about the work Keith did around the house; Keith would spend half a day a week on the house; and Keith and Shirley would spend another half-day together working on the house. At the same time Shirley would help with Keith's work, by keeping the accounts up to date.

Shirley and Keith went on to have another problem-solving session to discuss what tasks around the house had priority.

PRACTICAL EXERCISE

Negotiating Acceptable Requests

Set aside time to discuss your gripes.

Do	Do not
Make specific positive requests	Make vague or negative requests.

Show understanding and support for your partner's requests (i.e. validate).	Snap back that there is no way you will do that.
Level, when appropriate.	Hide your feelings or express them in a destructive way.
Use problem solving, if you disagree on how to change.	Remain in a stand-off.
Discuss one issue per session.	Try to solve all problems at once.

SWAPPING CHANGES TO ESTABLISH GOOD FAITH

It can be easier to motivate yourself to change if your partner is also trying to change at the same time. Then it doesn't feel that you are the only one trying. Seeing your partner trying to improve the relationship increases your faith in its future.

There are two ways you can go about helping each other to change. One is to swap changes, the other is to change in parallel.

Swapping changes can be simplest, and in fact is actually used by most couples. The couple are effectively making a contract, an agreement to exchange behaviours on the basis of good faith. 'If you do this, I will do that.' These swaps can be explicit, that is, the couple spell the exchange out, or they can be implicit, the couple both expect the exchanges to occur.

In the example above, Greg and Julie agreed to swap some behaviour changes.

Some examples of swapping behaviour changes:

'If you do the cooking, I'll do the washing up.'
'If you put the kids to bed, I'll make coffee.'
'If you make dinner tonight, I'll make dinner tomorrow night.'
'If you put the garbage out, I'll cook breakfast.'
'If you cook, I'll shop.'
'If you listen to me, I'll listen to your opinion.'

These contracts in a relationship generate feelings of trust and good faith. Both partners feel that their attempts to maintain the successful relationship will be reciprocated by the other partner.

In distressed relationships this good faith breaks down because the couple swap negative behaviours. Here are some examples of attempts to swap negative behaviours:

'You don't help me, so I won't help you.'
'You ignore me, so I won't cook you nice meals.'
'If you leave all the work to me, I won't do any.'
'If you knock me back when I initiate sex, I won't initiate it any more.'
'You never listen to me, so I will make sarcastic remarks about you in front of friends.'
'If you go out at night without telling me where you're going, I won't tell you where I am going.'

These attempts at swapping negative behaviours are very characteristic of distressed relationships. Each partner tries to force the other into changing some negative behaviour by threatening to match it with another negative behaviour. Each is trying to extract the maximum personal benefit from the other, but at the minimum personal cost. Although they may never be spelled out, these attempts to swap negative behaviours can become implicit contracts within the relationship.

If the relationship has developed many of these implicit, negative contracts, that is typically a sign that good faith and trust are breaking down. There are two practical implications of this. First, you should not set out to swap negative behaviours. That is only building more distress into your relationship. Only agree to swap changes that each would like to receive.

Second, if your relationship is spiralling down through exchanges of negative behaviours, a quick way to reverse this negative spiral is to swap positive behaviour changes.

For example, an implicit negative contract for Jenny and Martin had been: If Jenny acts jealously when Martin talks to another woman, Martin will ignore her and continue talking to the other woman.

This had increasingly become a problem. Jenny and Martin were tending to avoid going out together, because of this issue. After communicating about the problem, each expressing his and her feelings, they agreed upon this contract:

Jenny will react positively, if Martin smiles at her two or three times when he is talking to another woman.

This helped to restore the good feelings that Jenny and Martin had been losing. At the same time, they were able to go out together and enjoy themselves again.

Here are some common examples of swapping requests for behaviour change:

If you will cook three meals during the week, I will help you paint the house on Saturday.

If you ring me when you are going to be late, I will have your meal ready on time.

If you will pick the kids up from school, I will do the shopping.

If you comment nicely on my appearance at least once a week, I will entertain your business friends once a month.

If you will look at me three or four times during an evening with friends, I will smile back.

Remember, all the above contracts have only been made after the couple have used their communication skills to discuss the problem, and their problem-solving skills to agree upon how they will change.

Sometimes contracts to help you stop doing something can be used in emergencies, but notice that this is still swapping positive changes, not threatening each other with negative behaviours.

These contracts are useful for getting immediate change in an area that is causing a lot of disruption in the relationship, but they are only a temporary, stop-gap measure. They should not be used as a final solution to the problem. They are to help you get started on a particularly difficult or troublesome problem. Communication and problem solving still need eventually to occur. For example:

We both agree not to fight over this particular problem. We agree to use our skills to discuss it.

We both agree not to mention divorce until we have tried changing our relationship.

If you will stop nagging me about money, I will stop losing my temper and taking it out on you.

Behaviour-swap contracts can be a quick way of starting important changes in your relationship. But we leave you with a warning about behaviour-swap contracts. The basis of the contract is that you rely on the other person fulfilling their side of the contract before you are obliged to fulfil your side. This situation can very easily develop into a stand-off. The contract can become:

'If you do not fill your side of the contract first, I will not fill mine.'

You have the problem of who is going to go first. Our experience has shown that couples who get into these stand-off situations find them difficult to break, even with the help of a therapist.

Use the behaviour-swap form of contracting when it suits you. But the parallel form of contracting, which we describe now, does not have the trap of relying on the other person to fulfil the contract. Instead, you agree to make parallel changes in behaviour.

PARALLEL CONTRACTS

In a parallel contract, both partners agree to change some part of their behaviour, but those changes are independent of each other – they occur in parallel, rather than being swapped. In a sense, each partner says to the other, 'I will change this part of my behaviour as requested by you, as a sign of my good faith in the relationship, and not for any immediate payback of a change in you.'

This willingness to keep doing things for the good of the relationship, without there necessarily being any immediate payback, is characteristic of successful relationships. So you can see that parallel contracts help you to establish the pattern of behaviour change that usually occurs in successful relationships.

It is for this reason that we encourage couples to go on to parallel contracts, rather than staying with behaviour-swap contracts. Initially you may need to use behaviour-swap contracts to get some change started, and you may find them always suitable for simple problems. But later in working on your relationship, we suggest you move to using parallel contracts to strengthen the good faith in your relationship.

As with behaviour-swap contracts, you need to have gone through the process of communicating, defining problems, brainstorming, weighing up pros and cons, and then deciding upon a solution to try.

The best way to demonstrate this form of contracting is to give you some examples.

Parallel Contract 1

WIFE agrees to
Initiate one sexual intercourse with husband.

HUSBAND agrees to
Initiate and engage in one 20-minute conversation with six positive statements, (e.g., 'I never thought of that', 'That was interesting', 'That is a good idea', 'That is a new way of looking at it').

Engage in one sexual intercourse with husband.

Initiate and engage in one 20-minute period which will include affectionate behaviour like foot rubs and touching and patting.

Reward
One record album of wife's choice.

Reward
$6.00 worth of clothing.

Penalty
Do dishes for 3 days.

Penalty
Make lunches for 3 days.

Parallel Contract 2

WIFE agrees to
Initiate 3 ten-minute conversations with husband about husband's feelings, thought, etc. Conversation begins with an open-ended question by wife.

During the conversation wife keeps eye contact and makes comments on topic.

HUSBAND agrees to
During one occasion when company is present, husband will bring wife into conversation, make positive statements about her (e.g., 'That was interesting', 'That was a good idea') and do affectionate things to her (e.g., touch her hair, hold her hand, put his arm around her).

If child interrupts the conversation, wife acknowledges the interruption (e.g., 'I want to finish hearing this but . . .'), attends to child, then returns to the conversation. If the interruption is long, wife brings up the conversation later (e.g., 'I wanted to finish hearing about . . .')

Husband will do each of the above at least once but a total of five.

Reward
Two games of cards of wife's choosing.

Reward
During three consecutive mornings wife makes coffee or tea for husband.

Penalty
Wife picks up children's room and living room for three consecutive days.

Penalty
Husband does laundry once.

Parallel Contract 3

WIFE agrees to
Get up with husband and cook breakfast (3 mornings during the week).

HUSBAND agrees to
Pick kids up at Day Care on Monday night.

Watch kids while wife is in class Monday night.

Watch kids for 5 hours on Sunday.

Reward
One present costing $3.00 or less from husband.

Reward
One present costing $3.00 or less from wife.

Penalty
Sweep, vacuum, and dust.

Penalty
Wash and wax floor.

We the undersigned agree to the conditions of the above contract. We further agree to accept the partner's initiation of the above activities or suggest a more convenient alternate time.

WIFE: _____   HUSBAND: _____

DATE: _____

Let's see how these contracts for behaviour change work.

Make independent, specific requests

The behaviour each partner has agreed to change is completely independent of the other partner's behaviour changes. It is each partner's individual responsibility to change. Each has rewards and penalties completely separate from the other's behaviour change. Their contracts are in parallel, because they have rewards and penalties which do not depend on the other partner also changing.

Parallel contracting is less likely to produce stand-off situations, because each partner can be rewarded (or penalised) regardless of whether the other partner has kept his contract.

The requests for change are again couched in positive and specific terms. That is, the request for change is to increase or begin a specific, observable behaviour, by a specific amount. This reduces the risk of disputes occurring over whether the contract has or has not been kept.

If you find yourselves arguing over whether the changes you asked for have occurred, the problem may lie in your definitions of those changes. Go back to your contracts and make sure they are specific.

You will notice in the second example, the number of times the husband will speak to his wife is stipulated, as well as examples of the words he will say to her. This may seem silly at first. But imagine that this couple had not specified how often the husband was to make a conversation with his wife, or what he would say. An evening could pass where the husband thought he had said something to his wife a sufficient number of times but his wife may feel that he hasn't spoken to her enough. They would set themselves up for an argument.

In the first example contract, if the number of times the wife was to initiate sex was not specific, she may feel that initiating sex once a month was enough, while he may feel that twice a week was enough. They would also be setting themselves up for a dispute.

In parallel contracting, each partner is contracting with him or herself to change behaviours for the sake of the relationship. The rewards and penalties are just motivational aids, to help each partner keep his or her contract.

Rewards

Rewards can be money, a present you buy yourself, you can treat yourself to your idea of luxury, or you can ask your partner to do something for you. But it **must** be something your partner already does for you quite happily, or that your partner is happy to start doing. It should not be a request for behaviour change, or you are drifting back into behaviour swapping.

For example, you could not ask your partner to bring you a cup of coffee in bed in the morning as a reward for your behaviour change if your partner was reluctant to do this. However, if your partner was already willing to bring you coffee in bed in the morning, you could request this as your reward.

If you ask your partner to reward you by doing something you would like her to do and she refuses, you could always make that a later behaviour-change request.

For example, if you decided that a back rub from your partner was a good reward, but your partner was not already willing to do this, the next time you have a discussion on behaviour changes you could request that your partner gave you a back rub. Then you could negotiate on how often and when this occurred.

Penalties

You also set your own penalties. If you have chores you dislike doing, then these are ideal penalties.

Penalties can be everyday tasks that you normally have to do. The difference is that, when you use it as a penalty, you have to carry the task out whether it needs to be done or not.

For example, if you choose cleaning up the lounge room as a penalty, even if the room is clean, you have to clean it. Or if you choose mowing the lawns as a penalty, even if the lawns don't need mowing, you have to mow them. Penalties are meant to discourage you from forgetting your contract, so you have to apply them to yourself as soon as possible.

Making contracts

Try to make your rewards and penalties appropriate to the difficulty of your behaviour change. If the behaviour you have agreed to change is very difficult, then use large rewards and penalties. If you think the behaviour change is small, use small rewards and penalties.

Contracts don't have to be written out, like the ones in the examples, although this does have the advantage of avoiding later disputes over what was promised. If you are negotiating changes in a very difficult area, you may even want to sign the contract, like the couple in the third example.

Hang your contracts in a prominent position. Then, if there are any disputes over the contracts, you can refer to them. Hanging on the bedroom wall, or pinned to a kitchen cupboard, they are also reminders of the behaviour-change goals you have set for yourselves.

Some people find it helpful to record their behaviour changes. You can keep a simple tally: every time you are successful in changing your behaviour, give yourself a tick. At the end of the day or week, you have a clear record of your behaviour changes and you can reward or penalise yourself accordingly.

Example

John was trying to change the number of times he asked Andrea about something she was doing.

John and Andrea had agreed that once a day John would ask Andrea, 'How was your day?' or 'What have you been up to?' Andrea would respond, or thank John for asking her and suggest an alternate time to discuss her day if she was busy.

John kept a little graph inside his briefcase. The graph had two purposes: it reminded him to remember to ask Andrea about her day, and enabled him to keep a tally of his successes.

John's record looked like this:

	Week 1	Week 2	Week 3	Week 4
Monday	*		*	*
Tuesday	*		*	*
Wednesday	*	*		*
Thursday	*	*	*	*
Friday		*	*	*
Saturday			*	*
Sunday	*		*	*

John is beginning to change successfully. By the fourth week he has asked Andrea about her day, on every day of the week.

Ending contracts

You do not have to keep your contracts forever. They are only a means to an end. Once you feel that you have successfully changed your behaviour, or that you no longer need the motivational assistance of contracting with yourself, you can stop using that contract. This doesn't mean, of course, to forget about changing that behaviour. You can stop your contract when you are able to carry out your new behaviour fairly easily without needing to assist yourself.

If your contract doesn't work

If your contract doesn't seem to be working, set aside time to sit down with your partner and try to pinpoint why. It is not unusual to need to revise or adjust contracts.

Some guidelines to follow:

1 Have you defined the behaviour-change specifically enough? Can you see the behaviour, and count how often it occurs?

2 Do the rewards give you enough incentive to change?

3 Are your penalties too big, or not big enough?

4 What is your self-talk? Are you preventing yourself from changing? Is there a power struggle going on? Do you have a stand-off? An honest assessment of your self-talk may help you pinpoint problems like these. (Refer back to Chapter 5.)

5 Contracts should be reviewed, and changed if necessary. It can sometimes take a few trials before a contract really works. Spend some time and effort tailoring the contract to your own needs. This will maximise your chances of success.

Don't be put off by the apparent complexity of contracting. Like all tasks, it gets clearer when you actually try it, and easier with practice. So take the time **now** to prepare some appropriate behaviour-change contracts. Try both behaviour-swap and parallel contracts. If there are no issues in your relationship that need these skills now, make some up. It will be easier to negotiate changes in each other's behaviour when you need to, if you master the skills now.

FAIRY TALE

The Magic Pudding

(With apologies and acknowledgments to Norman Lindsay and Dr Claude M. Steiner)

Once upon a time, when we all lived in the Great Dreamtime long, long ago, everybody was happy, including the Smiths. Tim and Maggie Smith were very happy, living and loving together, and they were very happy with their two happy children, John and Lucy.

You see, in those days everybody was given, at birth, a Magic Pudding in a small bag, which they could easily carry around. Some people would even take their magic puddings to bed, to give each other slices.

This is because the puddings were magic in two ways. Firstly, whenever you ate a slice of Magic Pudding, it made you feel good. It wasn't like ordinary food (it didn't make you fat or anything like that) or drugs (it didn't affect your body at all). Because it was made entirely of good feelings, it just had this magical power of making you feel happy.

Secondly, no matter how many slices of your Magic Pudding you gave away, it never got any smaller. The more slices of your Magic Pudding you gave to other people, the more they would give to you. Because you had made them feel happy, they wanted to make you feel happy. So lots of Magic Pudding was being given away all the time, and everybody felt very happy.

Well, nearly everybody. There was one very unhappy person in the Great Dreamtime, and that was the Local Witch Doctor. He was very, very unhappy because everybody else was so happy that no-one ever came to buy his magic powders. He said his magic powders would make people feel happy, but the few people who tried them said they weren't nearly as good as Magic Puddings.

They didn't make you feel as happy as Magic Pudding did, they sometimes made you feel sick (which Magic Pudding never did), and they kept running out so you had to buy more from the Local Witch Doctor. Well, since people were quite happy to give each other Magic Pudding any old time, it wasn't surprising that no-one wanted even to try the Local Witch Doctor's magic powders.

The Local Witch Doctor may not have been happy, but he certainly was smart, in a cunning sort of way. So he worked out a Nasty Plan to get people to buy his magic powders.

One sunny afternoon, while Tim was relaxing under a tree feeling very good after Maggie had given him lots of her Magic Pudding, the Local Witch Doctor sneaked over and whispered in Tim's ear, 'You are being very childish, Tim. Look at all the Magic Pudding that Maggie is giving to John and Lucy. If she goes on like that, she'll run out and then she'll have none for you.'

Tim was astounded. He turned to the Local Witch Doctor and said, 'Do you mean her Magic Pudding could run out? I thought they lasted for ever!' Tim was very worried because he liked Maggie giving him Magic Pudding.

'Oh, don't be so silly', sneered the Local Witch Doctor, 'only a child would believe something like that! A grown-up would know that there isn't enough Magic Pudding to go around, and would be very careful not to waste it.'

Tim wasn't too sure why it was wrong to be like a child but, after all, the Local Witch Doctor was Educated and anyway he certainly didn't want to miss out on Maggie's Magic Pudding. He began to notice every time that Maggie gave a slice of her Magic Pudding to someone else. He became more and more worried. After all, he and Maggie were married, so it obviously wasn't right for her to waste her Magic Pudding on the children or other people.

So he started to complain every time he saw Maggie giving a slice of Magic Pudding to anybody else. Because Maggie loved Tim, she stopped giving Magic Pudding to others and saved it for him.

The children saw this and soon got the idea that it was wrong to give away Magic Pudding any time you were asked or felt like it. They too became very careful with their Magic Puddings. They watched their parents closely and whenever they felt that one of their parents was giving too much Magic Pudding to someone else, they would complain.

Soon their friends noticed how careful the Smiths were with their Magic Puddings, and they too began to worry about running out of Magic Pudding and so gave away less and less. Even though everybody's Magic Puddings never seemed any smaller, everybody worried that they might start to get smaller, and so they became meaner with their Magic Puddings.

To guarantee a steady supply of Magic Pudding, people would try to find someone to live with who would only give Magic Pudding to them alone, and never to anyone else. People who forgot themselves and gave some Magic Pudding to someone else would immediately feel guilty because they knew their partner would resent the loss of Magic Pudding.

Some people got so worried about running out of Magic Pudding that they would try to make their partners hand over slices without ever giving any back. They usually did this by complaining, 'You never give me any Magic Pudding so that proves you don't love me. You must give me some Magic Pudding before I give you any.'

Well, as you can guess, no-one was very happy any more, except for the Local Witch Doctor. He was very, very happy because more and more people started to buy his magic powders, trying to feel happy again. The powders didn't really make anyone feel very happy. 'But', they said, 'powdered happiness is better than none.'

However, the Local Witch Doctor's Nasty Plan had a snag in it. People started to feel so miserable they began to simply fade away. Well, people who faded away wouldn't be around to buy his magic powders, so the Local Witch Doctor had to change his Nasty Plan quickly.

The Nasty Plan (Second Version) went like this. The Local Witch Doctor set up a factory to make Plastic Puddings. These were fake Magic Puddings that looked a lot like the real thing, but were made from such heavy feelings that when you ate some, it stopped you from fading away.

At first, this looked as if it had solved the Local Witch Doctor's problem. People really wanted to feel good so they rushed to try the Plastic Puddings. But as soon as they found that eating Plastic Puddings only made you feel bad, they were even more miserable than before and started to fade away even faster. The Local Witch Doctor went back to his drawing board.

The Nasty Plan (Third Version) went like this. Next door to his Plastic Pudding factory, the Local Witch Doctor set up another factory that made Boxes. He tricked people into buying these Boxes and taking them home by saying that owning Boxes was a shortcut to feeling good again, because if you sat very still at home, staring at your Box and not saying anything to anyone, it would make you happy.

But instead of putting something in the Boxes that would really make people happy, the Local Witch Doctor filled them with messages about Plastic Puddings. Every time people sat and stared at their Boxes, they would see messages that told them that Plastic Puddings were as good as Magic Puddings. Some messages even said that the Plastic Puddings were 'NEW!' and 'IMPROVED!' and so were even better than Magic Puddings.

Well, people were so desperate to feel happy again that they went out and bought lots of Plastic Puddings in all sorts of shapes, colours and sizes. Some people believed that if they got lots of Plastic Puddings that would make them very happy. But of course, Plastic Puddings didn't make people happy; they just stopped you from fading away.

From time to time, some people would get so desperate trying to be happy with Plastic Puddings that they would buy more of the Local Witch Doctor's magic powders. This didn't help much, 'But', they said, 'I would probably feel worse without them.'

As you can see, things had got into rather a mess (except for the Local Witch Doctor, who was very, very, very happy selling lots of Plastic Puddings, Boxes and magic powders). When people got together, they would give each other Plastic Puddings. Because of what the Box had told them, they expected to make each other feel good by exchanging Plastic Puddings, so they were very confused when they felt bad.

The situation was very, very dismal and it had all started because the Local Witch Doctor had tricked people into believing that, if you freely gave away slices of your Magic Pudding of good feelings, one day it would run out.

A little while ago, something funny happened. A woman came to this unhappy land from somewhere else. Because she had never heard anything of the Local Witch Doctor's Nasty Plans, she didn't believe her Magic Pudding would ever run out, so she gave slices away to anybody.

Some people, who had grown up starved of Magic Pudding, thought this was great. They found that they too could freely give and receive Magic Pudding, although they were a bit frightened at first because of what they had been told in the past.

But some other people were shocked. They thought giving away lots of Magic Pudding was very reckless and unwise or even immoral. 'How childish and immature!' they said. 'Everyone knows that happiness depends on there not being enough of it.'

The Local Witch Doctor was very worried that, if people freely gave each other lots of Magic Pudding, no-one would want to buy his Plastic Puddings or Boxes or magic powders. So he put on his Local Witch Doctor's ceremonial robes and said very gravely, 'The only true path to happiness is through misery.'

He's still saying it, and he's still selling lots of Plastic Puddings and Boxes and magic powders, and people are still confused. Some people have discovered that they can give lots of Magic Pudding to their partners and their children and their friends and even to strangers, and there's no sign yet that their Magic Puddings are going to run out.

Some other people would like to share more Magic Pudding but they are scared by the stories they heard about Magic Puddings running out. And still others have been completely fooled by the messages they get from the Box and keep buying Plastic Puddings and magic powders and wondering why they don't feel good.

Right now, it's hard to guess how things will work out. Maybe more and more people will discover the truth about Magic Puddings. Or maybe people will always be too scared to share much of their Magic Puddings. Or maybe the Local Witch Doctor will come up with an Even Nastier Plan. What do you think?

8
Coping with kids

We had to laugh the other day at a bumper sticker we saw on the back of a station wagon, the interior of which resembled a cross between a toy box, a cafeteria, and a laundry. The sticker read: 'INSANITY IS HEREDITARY. YOU CATCH IT FROM YOUR CHILDREN'.

Like much humour, it was funny because it has a grain of truth in it. The popular myth is that children 'cement' a relationship, and parenting is one of the great rewards of marriage.

It's true that being a parent is often, perhaps even most of the time, rewarding and enjoyable. It's also true that being a parent can be demanding, dirty and destructive of relationships. Coping with the kids can be the straw that breaks the camel's back of a distressed relationship.

It's sad but not surprising that many people find parenting difficult. We began this book by discussing how little we are taught about human relations and how we cover up our lack of knowledge with myths about love and marriage. Equally we are taught little or nothing about how to bring up children and so invent another set of myths to hide our ignorance.

Modern-day parenthood has to cope with three problems that previous generations didn't have to face. First, there is the belief, largely arising from Freud and his followers, that childhood is a special formative period for your 'personality'. Childhood experiences are widely believed to leave marked or even unchangeable effects on the poor helpless infants suffering them. We'll debunk this myth shortly.

Second, many parents live in far greater social isolation

than before. People move home more often now, and family and friends may be geographically distant. Even those who do form good relationships with their neighbours may be reluctant to admit that they don't know what to do with their children. So good examples or advice are often in short supply.

This may seem an odd point of view given the number of books and courses on parenting being pushed by various 'experts' (and we are conscious of doing the same thing ourselves). But much of this advice is both so technical and so contradictory that it only results in confusing the poor parent even further. The only clear message is a reinforcement of the over-emphasis on childhood described above, and the parent's inadequacy to carry out this vital task.

The third characteristic of modern parenting can reinforce this sense of inadequacy. This is the rapid rate of change in the world around us. There is no doubt that the last part of the twentieth century is witnessing social, political, economic, industrial and environmental changes on a scale and at a rate never seen before. The tradition of parents handing down to their children the wisdom gained from their own experiences often no longer works. Mum and Dad grew up in a genuinely different world, and the skills and ideas that worked for them as kids may no longer meet the needs of their children.

This becomes most painfully obvious when your children reach adolescence. Teenagers are quick to point out, and increasingly with good cause, that you, the parent, can't know what it's like being a teenager now, and therefore can't usefully advise them on what to do. None of us likes to feel obsolete so many parents react hotly to these adolescent rejections of our wisdom.

As usually happens in heated conflicts, generation-gap arguments often result in throwing the baby out with the bathwater. The rebellious adolescent misses out on the good advice and support his parent has to offer. The stubborn parent drives her adolescent child away and minimises her chance of influencing his behaviour in sensible ways.

These three factors – an over-emphasis on the develop-mental importance of childhood, the social isolation of many parents, and the rapid changes in our world – have made more difficult a task that human beings have, after all, been doing with a modicum of success for some thousands of years. Our aim in this chapter is to give you some information and some practical advice to encourage you to believe that you too will probably be able to parent quite well.

Few parents are wilfully malicious or negligent. On the contrary, most parents are keen, perhaps too keen, to do the 'right thing' by their children. The trouble is that, for the reasons just described, many modern parents are uncertain or ill-advised as to what is the 'right thing'. When two parents have different ideas on what is 'right' for the children, you have the seeds of many conflicts.

One young couple we know had begun to argue over who should carry their baby in its bassinet. The young mother argued that her husband bumped the baby's head. The young father countered that his wife rocked the baby to and fro too much. The baby, who probably didn't care much who carried her bassinet, was only six weeks old and yet she had already become a source of repeated arguments between her parents!

It's unlikely and unnecessary that you should agree in every minute detail over your parenting. On the other hand, if there are big differences between you about what's expected from your children and how to handle them, that can make life difficult for the kids, especially if you argue over those differences.

When the kids in a family decide that one parent is 'softer' than the other on an issue, they may try to play you off against each other. 'Oh, go on Dad, Mum said we could.' Or, 'But Mum, Dad said we could go if you said it was all right.' These strategies can often lead to each parent feeling the other has let him or her down and then to more bad feelings in your relationship. Which doesn't do anyone in the family any good.

We are not suggesting that you should regard your children as the common enemy against whom you need to stand shoulder to shoulder. We are just saying that basic agreement between the parents on the main aspects of parenting makes it easier for your children to learn what's expected of them.

Just as you need a reasonable consistency between the two parents, there is a similar need for a reasonable level of consistency in your parenting over time. If your standards of acceptable kids' behaviour keep changing, it's pretty hard for your kids to know what's right.

Nor are we suggesting you should become a robot parent, programmed always to respond the same way. Like everybody else, you will have your crabby days when you are a bit unreasonable with your kids, and your mellow days when you are a bit soft. You and your kids will survive that much variability. It's the big and often unexplained changes in standards that kids find hard to handle.

It's also important to recognise that your expectations of your children should be age-appropriate. Don't expect a two year old to understand things the way a twelve year old might. Many parents make themselves unnecessarily upset by assuming that their toddlers, and even their babies, **intend** to make life difficult for them when the children don't really understand what's happening at all.

This need to make your expectations age-appropriate also means they should change as the ages of your children change. All parents would say that they would like to see their children eventually grow into being successful young adults, able to run their own lives independently. But many parents don't recognise that this goal means giving their children the chance to learn to run their own lives independently. This most often becomes a major problem when the children reach adolescence. Adolescents are keen to develop and try out their independence (although they usually also like to retain some parental support). Many parents find it difficult to let go of the expectations they had of their children as pre-teens, and accept more realistic ones.

In this book we have been encouraging you to question your expectations of your relationship by critically examining your beliefs about love and marriage and recognising when those beliefs are myths.

Now we want to encourage you to do the same for parenting, by reading and discussing the Myths of Parenthood below. These come from an excellent little self-help book, *Straight Talk to Parents*, by an American psychologist, Rian McMullin, published by the Colorado

Counseling Research Institute. We recommend it as further reading for any parents, but especially parents of teenagers.

THE MYTHS OF PARENTHOOD: OR HOW TO AVOID PREMATURE SAINTHOOD

Myth Number 1

'If I make a mistake, it will always affect my child.'

This myth has parents thoroughly rattled. 'Am I doing the right thing?' 'Will I hurt my child by being too soft (or too hard or too confused)?' It is based on the idea described above that childhood is a crucially important, formative phase of your life.

It surprises many people to learn that this is a very recent idea, popularised largely by Freud and his followers over the last eighty years. Like many of Freud's ideas, it is simply wrong. The Freudian notion that our adult 'personalities' are fixed by childhood experiences has been disproven. Some childhood experiences, particularly intense or repeated ones, naturally influence our later, adult behaviour. So do adolescent and adult experiences.

People **can** change how they act, think and feel at any stage in their lives, providing they want to, and are given the opportunity to. Which is probably just as well, or we psychologists would be out of business. There is no evidence that childhood experiences are more important or formative than later ones.

The only real effect of this myth has been to make parents over-anxious about their parenting. Now we encourage you to get it into perspective. Children have many influences on them. Parents are usually one significant influence, but by no means the only one.

A good example of this, although it is one which frustrates many parents, is the situation where parents have tried to show healthy attitudes towards nudity to their children. The parents have not discouraged naturally occurring nudity around the home and don't believe that their bodies are 'dirty' or 'shameful'. Then suddenly, and disappointingly, the kids become awkward and embarrassed over what has been such a natural part of home life. Bathroom doors are locked, and parents may be asked to wear a dressing-gown on the way to the bathroom. What has happened, of course, is that your children are now being influenced by their friends or teachers or what they have read or watched on television.

Like every other parent, you will occasionally make a 'mistake'. You will do something that distresses your child, or something that later you may wish you had done differently. Such a mistake will only be one of many experiences, one of many influences on your child. On the other hand, worrying all the time about **maybe** making a mistake as a parent will only make you anxious and more likely to make a real mistake.

Children rarely learn anything, including your mistakes, in one go. They generally cope with bad feelings better than adults do. How often have you seen a child bawling her head off one minute, and laughing happily the next? Your children may be **distressed** by something you do, including your parenting mistakes, but that does not necessarily mean they will be **harmed** by the experience.

Of course, we are not saying this about on-going physical or psychological abuse. That is a very different matter. Parents who abuse their children are often reacting in understandable ways to intolerable pressures. Because child abuse is regarded, quite properly, as unacceptable behaviour, many child abusers feel extremely guilty and keep their problem secret.

Saying that child abuse is usually 'understandable' is not meant to excuse it, only to imply that it is a problem which can often be helped. If you ever find yourself in this situation, don't hide it from yourself. For your own sake, and that of your children, seek professional help immediately.

Myth Number 2

'As a parent, I have the power to make my kids do whatever I want.'

The only behaviour control method that we know works is a double-barrelled shotgun, held 15 centimetres from the head of the person you want to control, or some similar threat to life and limb. Such threats work only as long as they are present, and are typically part of fearful and coercive relationships.

What most of us can do in most of our relationships is **influence** the way other people behave, not control it. Sometimes there is an illusion of control, because the other person accepts your influence or chooses to behave as you would want, for her own reasons. But the illusion becomes apparent when she decides not to accept your influence, and to behave in some other way, for her own reasons.

The illusion that parents can control their children's behaviour is fed by two factors. First, children start out being very small, so they can be scared into doing what their parents want by threatening them with physical violence, including the traditional smack on the bottom. The illusion here is revealed when the kids get big enough to hit back!

Second, children start out very emotionally dependent on their parents. They want to love you, and you to love them. So for a while they can be scared into doing what you want by your threats of withholding your love. The illusion here is revealed when they give up trying to have a satisfactory love relationship with you, sometimes by looking elsewhere for love, sometimes by giving up on love altogether.

You will have noticed that the illusion of behaviour control is based on threats of physical or emotional hurt. If you decide to try to achieve control of your children's behaviour, don't be surprised if they become frightened of you, and eventually dislike you. If you stand over your child and force him to do something, then you may have temporary control over him but you will not control his thoughts, feelings and future actions. The only control you have over him is when you are present. This is a very ineffective way of teaching. Good teaching eventually encourages your children to continue with the behaviour by themselves.

Sometimes control becomes an issue because the parents have certain goals in mind for their children. A parent may want his child to achieve all the things that he didn't manage to achieve for himself. Or he may believe his child should be successful like him, and therefore be a carbon copy of him. The fact that you biologically created your child, and have provided her with basic care or even love, does not give you the right to control her destiny. Attempting to do so usually creates frustration for the parent and resentment in the child.

Naturally, it's fine for you to encourage your child in the pursuit of general goals of success and happiness, but it's crucial for your relationship with him that you let him decide just what constitutes success or happiness.

Because many people believe the myth of parental control of children, they believe that the parents are responsible for the children's behaviour. So if the children behave badly, that is supposed to reflect on the parents. How often have you seen a parent scolding a child largely because the parent is embarrassed by the child's behaviour?

We encourage you to see through this myth. You are responsible for influencing your children to behave sensibly and responsibly, but you cannot make them. So it's a bit silly to blame yourself for their occasional choice to behave badly.

We are **not** suggesting you sit back and let your children do what they like, regardless of the danger or nuisance involved. We are suggesting you set as your broad goal, influencing your children's behaviour, not controlling it. Later we'll describe some techniques for maximising your influence.

Myth Number 3

'My children cause all my unhappiness. They must change how they behave for me to feel better.'

You are responsible for your own feelings. How you feel about things is largely determined by how you think about them, and your thoughts are under your control. Other people's actions can influence how you feel, but how you interpret and respond to those actions is your responsibility.

Sometimes other people, and their behaviour, can be a convenient scapegoat for your bad feelings. For example, you have had a bad day, the kids start to play noisily in the evening, and you shout at them for 'making' you feel bad. Of course, you can request behaviour changes from your children, like playing more quietly or in another room, just as you can request behaviour changes from each other. But you can also check your own self-talk in the situation to see how realistic you are being about the source and solution of your bad feelings.

Later we will indicate how many of the relationship skills you have been learning to use with each other also work very well in your relationships with your children. And that includes taking responsibility for your own self-talk and feelings.

You chose to go into your relationship, and you chose (more or less, we hope) to make babies. Babies never choose to be made. If your children really are an intolerable burden to you, let them live with some substitute parents who really want them. This may seem drastic, but it is occasionally the best solution for both the unwilling parents and the unwanted children.

Myth Number 4

'Children are naturally undisciplined and behave like wild animals. Parents must beat them into shape to make them civilised.'

There are two false beliefs in this myth. First, there is the idea that children are 'naturally bad'. As we said earlier, humans do very little 'naturally', because from birth onwards they are learning, including what behaviours are successful and acceptable under what circumstances.

If the only way your child can successfully get your attention is by playing up noisily, don't be surprised if she plays up a lot. If your child discovers that throwing tantrums usually means that he gets what he wants, don't be surprised if he throws lots of tantrums.

If your child has unfortunately learned to behave in ways that you don't like, your first task is to identify what influences, including your own behaviour, are encouraging her to act like that. Once you know what these influences are, you are halfway towards influencing her to change her behaviour. More on how to do that later.

The second false belief in this myth is that punishment is a good way of stopping people from doing things. Our culture has an elaborate mythology about punishment, all of it basically saying that punishment is an effective way of changing behaviour. Many of those who dole out punishment – parents, teachers, courts – don't like hearing this idea questioned.

But there is now a lot of research on the effects of punishment in humans, and it all seriously questions the popular beliefs about punishment. As soon as we say this to groups of parents or teachers, the usual response is for us to be told how people remember behaving themselves because they were frightened of being punished. 'See, it worked for us, so it should work for our children.'

A couple of questions to the same group will always establish that the same people also remember how many times they 'got away with it'. They can easily remember how punishment only works some of the time.

We can summarise that research by saying that, if punishment is reliably going to stop a person from doing something, it must be very severe; it must follow immediately after the unwanted behaviour every time it occurs; and it should be administered by someone that the offender feels close to.

Even if you were able to achieve these requirements – and ask yourself how likely it is that you would always catch your kids playing up – punishment has two negative side effects, social and motivational.

The recipient of punishment typically feels resentful towards the punisher, and shows increased aggression after being punished. If he can't direct this aggression towards his punisher, he may direct it towards some person or object he sees as associated with the punisher, or towards some unrelated person or object. Have you ever wondered why so many kids burn down schools? Or why so many kids are physically violent towards other kids?

Punishment is essentially telling the person to stop behaving. It provides neither information nor encouragement for more acceptable behaviour. Punishing your child for misbehaving may stop her from behaving that way, at least temporarily, but it won't by itself get her to behave better.

The truth is that punishment is not a good way of changing behaviour – its effects are unreliable and don't last for long. Humans are much more influenced by rewards.

More effective ways of changing human behaviour that do not have the negative side effects of punishment involve rewarding desirable behaviour, and removing the rewards of undesirable behaviour. We'll explain some techniques for doing both of these later.

We are not saying you must never punish your children, or that you should feel dreadfully guilty when you do. We are saying that punishment is most helpful when it is consistent, and is accompanied by information as to why that particular behaviour is unacceptable, along with information about and the opportunity for more desirable behaviour, which is rewarded when it occurs.

Myth Number 5

'It is my responsibility to solve my children's problems.'

It is easy to be tempted to save your child from being hurt, physically or emotionally. After all, seeing him hurt or distressed is hurtful or distressing for you. But that's exactly the problem in this myth.

When you rescue your child, is it because of a real threat to his well-being or safety, or is it to protect your own feelings?

Do you feel embarrassed if other kids tease your kid?

Do you exaggerate the dangers of situations because of your own fear?

Do you feel a sense of failure if your child doesn't do well at something?

We are not suggesting you ignore your children's well-being or safety. We are suggesting that you draw a line between situations which genuinely threaten your child, and situations which are more threats to your feelings about being a 'good' parent.

As we said above, parents will usually want to see their children as eventually becoming successful, independent adults. Again, this logically means your children must have the chance to learn what is successful, and how to be independent.

You can certainly help your child tackle her problems, by offering advice, assistance and support. The younger she is, the more advice or assistance she may need. But you sabotage your own long-term goal for your child as soon as you take over her responsibility for solving her problems.

Imagine trying to explain to a visitor from outer space what chocolate icecream is like. You could describe the colour, the flavour, the texture, the temperature. You could even give them its chemical formula. But the only way they would really know what it's like would be to try it.

You can give your child lots of information and advice, and warnings when they are appropriate. But the only way he will eventually really understand what the world is about, and how to cope with it, will be to taste it for himself.

PRACTICAL EXERCISE

Read the myths and our discussion above independently, and then discuss them together, asking much the same questions as before:

How much have these myths influenced our expectations about parenting?

What can we agree now are our realistic expectations of parenting?

SOME PRACTICAL GUIDELINES TO PARENTING

We will now describe some practical procedures to use in your parenting, beginning with some general rules of thumb, and then outlining procedures to use with young children, and finally some procedures to use with teenagers.

Four rules of thumb

1 Be consistent.
Try to be consistent in your dealings with your children. Give yourselves permission to have typical variations in your own moods and responses, and typical differences of opinion between you. But recognise that it's easier for your children to learn what's expected of them if those expectations are reasonably consistent.

If you find there is a major difference between you in your expectations of the children, that's a target for your communication and problem-solving skills.

2 Give unconditional love.

The only kind of love worth giving or receiving is unconditional love. It is the love which says, 'I love you as a person. Sometimes I may dislike some of your behaviour, and that may lead to bad feelings between us, but it does not reduce my love for you.'

This does not mean that you feel love for the other person all of the time. We all occasionally get bored or angry with each other. It does mean that you draw a clear distinction between your regard for the other person and your regard for her behaviour.

As we discussed above, some parents unfortunately threaten or use the withdrawal of their love to try to control their children's behaviour. Effectively they are saying, 'I will only love you **if** you do what I want.'

Children who grow up with conditional love often have difficulty in later love relationships, because they have never learned to value themselves as people, rather than achievers.

3 Use trial-and-success learning.

There is no such thing as trial-and-error learning. Mistakes and failure discourage people. All you learn from an error is that you are wrong. Fail often enough, and you give up trying.

Success tells you that you have found the right answer. It encourages you to keep trying. The more you have succeeded in the past, the more you will tackle new problems and the harder you will try.

It is important that you have realistic expectations of your children. It is unrealistic to expect anyone to do anything difficult right the first time. It is realistic only to expect that he will **try** his best; this may or may not be successful.

If you would like your child to be a trier, then reward his efforts, not just his successes. We are not suggesting that you go overboard and reward or praise everything your child does. Rewards that come too easily don't mean much. We are suggesting that you are realistic about what you call a success and give a reward.

Children who grow up with praise don't develop swelled heads. They become confident adults.

4 Use your relationship skills.

Unless you never see each other, you will have relationships with your children, just as you have with each other. Your communication skills, fight control skills and problem-solving skills can be adapted quite well to parent-child relationships.

Of course, your adaptation needs to be age-appropriate. A young child may not yet be able to validate your feelings because she may not fully understand your levelling. Give her time. What better place could there be for her to learn effective communication skills than in her relationship with you?

She may also not be able to contribute much to a problem-solving session yet. But the active consideration of her feelings and wishes, and the obvious weighing up of possible solutions, can help her to accept a decision that is different from what she wanted.

Parallel to coupling, we can talk about 'familying' – doing good things together as a family, or at least one parent sharing something good with one or more of the children. Like coupling, familying is essential if you want to make and keep good feelings in your relationships with your children.

Fathers are particularly at risk of neglecting their relationships with their children while they are young, partly because they have accepted old sexist myths about child-rearing being 'women's work', and partly because they are busy establishing themselves in a job or career.

It is sad to hear from these fathers later how disappointed they are that they aren't closer to their children. It's never too late to try to bridge such a gap. Providing parent and child both want to, you can always start familying. Adapt the guidelines for coupling; they fit quite well.

Just as you will have had to make a very deliberate effort to introduce the basic relationship skills into your relationship with each other, it takes just as conscious an effort to do it with your children. Similarly, this may sometimes be a rather self-conscious effort. Wear it; there are no terminal cases of embarrassment, and it's a small price to pay for better relationships in the whole family.

HELPING YOUNG CHILDREN CHANGE THEIR BEHAVIOUR

If you think that your young child, say less than twelve, is behaving in some ways you don't like, here are some basic steps to help him stop behaving in ways you don't want, and start or increase behaving in ways you do want.

These brief guidelines should be enough for you to implement a behaviour-change programme with your child. If you would like more detailed self-help, we have listed some good books at the end of this chapter. If your problem seems beyond self-help, or you try it and it doesn't work, do seek the help of a properly trained psychologist.

Step 1 Define the problem

Using the ideas we have already discussed, try to define precisely what your child does or doesn't do that is a problem. Again, be sure you are pinpointing actual behaviours, and not your interpretations of them.

Think about whether the problem lies in your child's behaviour, or your feelings about it. Review the Myths of Parenthood above. Discuss the problem with your partner, and see whether you agree there is a real problem here. You will both need to take part in any behaviour-change programme, if you agree one is needed. Even very young children will understand what you are saying to them, although you will have to follow up what you say consistently with your actions each and every time the problem occurs. Most children's concentration span is very short and you will have to be prepared to repeat yourself patiently and consistently.

Step 2 Count the behaviour

If you want your child's behaviour to change, you need a marker of what it was like before your programme, so that you can tell if it is changing. This is one of the reasons that you need a precise definition of the problem: it must involve observable behaviour that you can record, just as your behaviour-change requests of each other do.

It often helps to keep a tally, or a graph, of the problem behaviours, so that all can see changes as they occur.

For example, you may have started with the gripe that your child is disobedient. This leads you to define two precise behaviours: you would like your child more often to accept your reasonable requests, and you would like your child less often to ignore or disobey your reasonable requests.

For each day, count the number of times he complies with your requests, and the number of times he ignores or disobeys your requests. You could keep a chart on his bedroom wall, showing both totals for each day. If you like, you can draw two graphs, one for each score.

	Requests ignored	Requests complied with
Mon.	* * * *	*
Tues.	* *	* *
Wed.	* * *	*
Thurs.	* *	*
Fri.	* *	*
Sat.	*	*
Sun.	* *	*

Sometimes when you begin monitoring, the behaviour you wish to change will begin to decrease. This won't last, so keep up the programme.

Behaviours are often not easy to define. For example how do you define a tantrum? Is it when your kid is yelling and kicking, or is it when she slams the door in anger? Be sure you all agree on the definition of the behaviour you are changing.

You may also find that the behaviour you thought was a problem isn't. You may have thought your son teased your daughter a lot, but when you recorded his behaviour you saw that it only happened about once a week, particularly when he was tired, so the teasing was not really the problem.

Step 3   Identify rewards and penalties

First, are there any apparent rewards that are supporting unwanted behaviours? For example, do you only pay attention to him when he disobeys you? Your attention is one of the most powerful rewards in your child's life. Even your angry attention is better than none.

If there are apparent rewards for misbehaving, try to eliminate them. If your attention has been a reward, give only as much as is needed to implement the programme, but remember to give plenty when he behaves properly.

Second, what is a suitable reward for changing his behaviour? A good rule of thumb here is that anything he does a lot of is likely to be rewarding. So, if he rides his bike a lot, that could be a suitable reward. Try to match the 'size' of the reward to the difficulty of the behaviour-change.

Third, what is a suitable penalty for not changing his behaviour? Sometimes the natural consequences of doing something silly are enough of a penalty themselves, providing you don't overprotect your child from them. Sometimes you will need to set up a suitable penalty, usually a loss of some privilege, like watching television, or a reduction in pocket money.

Step 4 Contract for the desired behaviour-change

In a roundtable discussion involving the child and preferably both parents, agree on the behaviour-change goals: strengthening desirable behaviours; eliminating undesirable behaviours. Write out a clear contract.

For example, for each day that Charlie obeys reasonable requests from his parents, he gets one star on his chart. At the end of the week, if he has at least six stars, Dad will take him bike-riding in the local park. On any day that Charlie doesn't obey reasonable requests, he loses half an hour television time.

Pin up the contract where it can be seen, as a reminder of the desired behaviour-change, and so that there is no room for argument about what was promised.

CONTRACT FOR EATING DINNER AT NIGHT

John agrees to eat all his dinner every night.

He will be given a tick on his chart each night he eats his dinner. He will be given a cross on his chart each night he does not eat his dinner.

Reward: John can choose his favourite dessert.
           When John has 20 ticks he can go roller skating.

Penalties: Each time John gets a cross he has to tidy up the toys
in his room.

Step 5 Try out the contract

Don't be surprised if your child first tries to buck the contract.
You are taking away some of the influence he has had over
you! Stick to the contract. The most common reason for this
procedure not working is the parents' being inconsistent.
Once you break the contract, don't be surprised if your child
tries to.

Review how the contract is going from time to time. It is
not unusual to need to revise a contract. The behaviour-
change specified, or the reward or penalty, may have been
too big or too little. If you are aiming for a large behaviour-
change, you may need to use several contracts, each of which
is a step along the way.

Make whatever changes are necessary in more roundtable
discussions.

Step 6 Fade out the contract

Your long-term goal is for your child to develop self-control
and self-discipline. Contracting is a short-term measure to
aid that development. There are two basic ways of fading
contracts.

First, you can gradually raise your standards for a reward,
so that the desired behaviour becomes less and less dependent
on immediate reward. Of course, you should still reward
desirable behaviour with your attention and praise.

Second, if the child is old enough to do this, you can shift
control of the contract to her. In the beginning, you count the
behaviour, keep the records, and hand out the rewards.
When the contract is working, hand over the counting and
record-keeping to your child.

Don't worry: research shows that the kids are usually much
tougher on themselves than the adults have been. When this
procedure is running well, hand over control of the rewards
as well.

Tell your child that she can forget the contract when she
thinks she no longer needs its help to keep up the behaviour-
change. You might like to agree on some other way she can

still earn her rewards, such as by doing a household chore, so that she isn't losing out for solving the problem.

QUESTION: HOW DO I REASON WITH AN UNREASONABLE CHILD? ANSWER: YOU DON'T!

Behaviour is most easily and effectively changed by intelligent use of rewards, as we have just outlined. It works best when the child is involved in the whole process, and the contract is seen as an aid to his changing his behaviour in ways that make everybody happier, if only by reducing conflict and hostility.

This means that the child has to be willing to take part in the discussion and to try out the contract. This means the child has to be willing to be reasonable, at least most of the time.

Sometimes children, like adults, are not reasonable. They are so upset, or angry, or cranky, that no reasonable appeal from you is acceptable to them. These are the circumstances that really try a parent's patience. The parent who says she has never felt like hitting her kids is probably lying.

We have discussed above why punishment based on physical or emotional violence isn't the best answer to children's unreasonable behaviour. Instead, we suggest a non-violent form of punishment called Time Out.

We use Time Out in fight control to give both partners time to cool down so that they can act more constructively (see Chapter 5). In parent-child relationships Time Out can be used in much the same way. The child is given Time Out from the interaction with the parent, and from all rewarding and interesting activities. This gives the child (and sometimes the parent) time to cool down, so that he can act more reasonably. It also represents an effective punishment because the child loses your attention and access to anything rewarding.

Time Out can take a little time and effort to implement, particularly with children who have already learned skilled disruptive behaviours, like tantrums. Again, you should not be surprised if your child tries to buck the system when it is first introduced. Be consistent and you will be surprised by how quickly you can eliminate some really undesirable behaviour.

Here are the steps for using Time Out with children.

Step 1 Choose a Time Out location

This should be somewhere boring and uninteresting. Bedrooms often don't work, because your child has toys and other interesting things there, although sometimes just the loss of your company is punishing enough. Some families find the bathroom works best. If there are possibly interesting things around, like bottles of shampoo, keep them in a plastic box which can easily be removed.

Time Out is **not** meant to be frightening. **Don't** lock the child in a room. **Do** switch on a light, if it is dark.

Step 2 Explain Time Out to the child

Tell her exactly what she does that is unacceptable, and why it is unacceptable. Explain that in the future, if she behaves that way, she earns Time Out. This means going to the Time Out place for the amount of time specified by you.

Time Out does not need to be long to be effective. Research has found that four minutes works as well as forty, and it is a lot easier to administer. If you have a wind-up kitchen timer, you can tell your child that she can come out from Time Out when the timer rings.

The exception to this rule of thumb is when the undesirable behaviour continues in Time Out. For example, the child may be sent to Time Out for throwing a tantrum, and he may continue to scream while there. Then he is told that he may come out after he stops screaming. Always make clear the conditions for coming out of Time Out.

Step 3 Implement Time Out

Be consistent. There is often a little burst of the undesirable behaviour at first while the child tries out the new procedure (and you).

Never take your child to Time Out by force. That's only substituting one kind of violence for another. If he refuses to go, calmly add another minute to his Time Out. If adding several minutes to Time Out doesn't do the trick, you may back it up with another penalty, like a loss of privileges.

A word of caution:

Contracting and Time Out have been repeatedly shown to be effective techniques for parents to use in coping with the 'normal' problems of 'normal' children, so long as the parents employ them consistently. They will not solve more serious problems that children occasionally develop.

If you try these procedures, and you think you really have tried them properly and consistently but your child's behaviour does not improve, do see a properly trained psychologist.

RESOLVING PARENT-ADOLESCENT CONFLICTS

As we discussed earlier, adolescence is a period in which your children will want to develop their independence in preparation for their adult lives and this often results in conflict between the adolescent and her parents. To be frank, much of that conflict is really unnecessary and results largely from the parents still buying into the myths discussed above. Does it really matter how long your son's hair is, or how short your daughter's dress is? Both may lead to your feeling uncomfortable, but that's your responsibility.

We are not suggesting you take no interest in your teenager's activities or that you condone anything he does. We are suggesting that by this stage it is all the more important that you recognise that you cannot control your children's behaviour, and that you have a much better chance of influencing it if you use your relationship skills.

If you think there is unnecessary conflict between you and a teenage child, sit down and discuss it together in a roundtable discussion. Use your communication skills, and give your teenager the chance to learn them. Let him read the appropriate chapter in this book, and then show you are willing to validate his point of view, without necessarily agreeing with it.

Keep the Myths of Parenthood in your mind. Are your gripes about his behaviour real problems? If you decide they are, use your problem-solving skills. Again, let him read the appropriate chapter, and show you want him to take an active part in working out a solution that suits all of you.

We see many more families with parent-adolescent conflict involving daughters than sons. At first this may seem surprising, since traditionally we expect boys to be the ones who play up. But that's exactly the reason for this discrepancy. Parents seem to be more likely to be over-protective, and therefore over-restrictive, towards their adolescent daughters than sons. There is some reason for this: daughters can get pregnant, sons can't.

But there is nothing, we repeat, nothing, you can stop your daughter from doing, short of actually imprisoning her. You have your best chance of influencing her to behave sensibly if you have a close relationship, based on mutual trust and respect. You minimise your chances of influencing her behaviour if you have an antagonistic relationship based on your lack of trust and respect for her, expressed through futile attempts to control her behaviour.

WHOSE CHILDREN ARE WHOSE?

With the growing number of second and third marriages in our community, there are a growing number of families with children of mixed parentage: some from previous marriages, some from this marriage. The position may be further complicated by visits to or by an absent parent.

These mixed families can suffer from particular problems. Older children from a previous marriage may feel threatened by younger children from the new relationship. One of the partners in the relationship may feel uncertain about relating to the other partner's children from a previous marriage, especially in matters of discipline.

We can't deal with this situation at length here, but the following are some tips that we have found helpful for mixed families.

If you are suddenly a 'new' parent, don't expect to replace the old one. Your 'new' children, unless they are very young, will know who you are, and can form quite satisfactory relationships with you on that basis. Don't rush this process:

use the parenting skills described above to develop good relationships over time.

It is especially important that the two adults have discussed their expectations of parenting, and reached broad agreement. You may have to back each other up if a child tries to play off an 'old' parent against a 'new' one. Again, the child benefits in the long run from this consistency.

An 'old', non-custodial parent should recognise that the custodial parent and his or her new partner have accepted prime responsibility for the children's care, and therefore should have the major say. Ideally, the non-custodial parent should be able to express an opinion, but the final say belongs to the custodial parent.

It goes without saying that the non-custodial parent should not be sabotaging the custodial parent's efforts, even if he or she doesn't agree with them. Such sabotage is often a cheap attempt at revenge for past hurts, and reveals an utter disregard for the children's wellbeing.

In principle, biological relationship is unimportant, as has been shown by the successful relationships developed in adopting families, or where artificial insemination has been used, with sperm from an anonymous donor. Biological kinship has only the importance you give it, which is your self-talk.

Make reasonable allowances for reasonable feelings, but don't let the presence or absence of a biological relationship be used as a red herring to hide issues that arise, and can be solved, in any family.

NORMAL PROBLEMS IN NORMAL CHILDREN – SUMMARY APPROACHES

We often find that parents can apply a set of guidelines to solve one problem with their children, but they find it difficult to generalise these techniques to other problems. To avoid this we have set out brief guidelines below for solving normal problems in normal children.

You can use these guidelines like a cookbook, just look up what you wish to change in your child, refer to the detailed method in this chapter, and then follow the recipe.

Non-compliance
Contract for compliance (including graph of successes), Time Out for non-compliance.

Teasing
Contract for not teasing (including graph of success), Time Out for teasing.

Toilet training in the 3 year old
Contract for bathroom use (including graph of successes), make child responsible for rinsing training pants. **Do not** scold or punish.

Bed wetting
Contract for dry bed (including graph of successes), make child responsible for changing wet bedding. **Do not** scold or punish.

Temper tantrums
Contract for compliance (including graph of successes), Time Out for tantrums.

Child in parents' bed
Contract for staying in own bed (including graph of successes).

Whining
Contract for not whining (including graph of successes), Time Out for whining.

Going to bed
Contract for going to bed (including graph of successes), Time Out for not going; use a 30-minute signal for approaching bed-time.

SOME SELF-HELP RESOURCES FOR PARENTING

Five Practical Guides to Changing Children's Behaviour, Howard Sloane: *Because I Said So, Dinner's Ready, No More Whining, Stop that Fighting*, How-to Publications; *Not 'til Your Room's Clean*, Telesis Ltd, 1976.

For teenagers
How to Put Up with Parents, Thomas Gnagey, Facilitation House, 1975.

For parents and teachers
Little Changes Mean a Lot, How to Improve the Behaviour

of Children and Other Important People, Marcia McBeath, Prentice-Hall, 1979.

For parents
Living with Children, New Methods for Parents and Teachers, Gerald Patterson, Research Press, 1976.
Straight Talk to Parents, Rian McMullin, Colorado Counseling Research Institute, 1978.
Surviving with Kids, Wayne Bartz and Richard Rasor, Impact Publishers, 1978.

9

What to do if it all doesn't work

SEPARATE, DIVORCE, OR SEE SOMEONE?

It is not chiselled on a piece of stone, anywhere, that you and your partner were predestined and preordained to have a successful relationship. It is not a sign of great personal failure if you finally decide you are in the wrong relationship (regardless of what your mother may tell you).

About a third of the couples we see for marital therapy eventually decide to separate, and our impression is that this is the best outcome of therapy for them. They have decided to call it quits on their relationships for the only good reason: the relationship can't be made to work satisfactorily.

There are plenty of spurious reasons for quitting relationships. One of the partners has had an affair, or they have had a big argument ending with one partner walking out, or they don't feel in love any more. These are the common symptoms of a distressed relationship, not evidence that it can't be put right.

The only way you can be reasonably sure your relationship can't work is to try honestly and constructively to make it work. That's what good relationship therapy, and this book, are about. If you have both given it a reasonable try, and it still isn't working, then that is information that you should act on.

It is our impression that relationships decline steadily, not in great jumps. Up to a certain point, it is possible to reverse that decline if both partners are willing to work together to make the relationship better.

Inside Woody Allen

But there seems to be a point of no return in this decline after which it is not possible to rebuild the relationship. This seems to occur because one or both of the partners have lost faith in the relationship. They no longer believe in the good intentions and feelings of each other, and therefore they no longer believe the relationship can work.

This loss of trust in the relationship typically results in a holding back from active commitment. One partner may try to improve communication, or coupling, or whatever, but the other partner responds reluctantly, if at all. He just doesn't believe it's worth trying any more.

The realistic choice for couples who reach this point is to separate. The difficulty for many couples is deciding whether they have reached this point. Nearly all separating couples feel ambivalent about their decision when they finally act on it, regardless of how distressed their relationships have been.

These mixed feelings have two common causes. First, the partners are usually not sure that they have really given their relationship a proper chance to work. They will have self-talk like: 'But what if we did (or had) . . . ' or 'If only we did (or had) . . . '

Second, one or both of the partners may be scared of losing the support and security of the relationship, no matter what else was wrong with it. This fear is an expression of that person's low self-esteem: 'If I lose this relationship, I could never possibly find another, so I had better hang onto this one, no matter how bad it is.'

The only answer to the first reason for staying in a bad relationship is genuinely to try to make it better. This book sets out a self-help programme, which is intended to help make that effort easier. If you believe you have tried our self-help steps as well as possible, and your relationship has not improved enough to be really satisfactory, then that outcome is information you should act on.

On the other hand, self-help is not for everyone. It is particularly difficult for couples who fight a lot because the self-help programme can become something more to fight over. In any case, we believe that relationship therapy is one of the most difficult tasks for a well-trained professional, so it isn't surprising that many couples find it hard to do it for themselves.

If you try self-help for your relationship and it doesn't work, or if reading this book makes you balk at the idea of trying self-help, don't despair. It may mean that you should seek the assistance of a well-trained counsellor or therapist.

Remember that there are horses for courses. In our experience, volunteer counsellors – non-professional people who have some limited training in counselling – can provide a valuable sympathetic ear and some basic advice to people whose troubles are not too great. But if the problems are complicated, or long entrenched, then we believe you need the technically skilled advice of a properly trained professional. The sad truth is that this can be hard to find in Australia, but as a rule of thumb we recommend a psychologist who is a member of the clinical board of the Australian Psychological Society, or who has a postgraduate university qualification in clinical psychology.

Beware of imitations. In any case, if you don't feel you are getting concrete help after a couple of consultations, we suggest you change helpers. We encourage people to become discriminating consumers of health and helping services.

Sorting out the second reason for staying in a bad relationship can be more difficult. It is obviously painful to have to admit to yourself that the only reason you are staying in your present rotten relationship is because you have such a low opinion of yourself that you doubt that you could either cope by yourself or find a better relationship.

You may have to face up to this possibility if you have eliminated the first, by really trying to work on the relationship but without success, and yet you find yourself clinging on. If you think this does apply to you, set yourself two tasks.

Find out about separation and divorce. Get legal advice about what to do and what your rights are. Talk to someone who has been through it all. Diminish your fear of the unknown by making it at least partly known.

At the same time, ask yourself, 'What would I do if my partner was suddenly killed in an accident?' Most people we have put that question to decide that they would be hurt, would grieve for their lost partners, and then they would survive. Most will even agree that they might eventually form new relationships, and that these new relationships might even be better than the ones they are in now.

Separation and divorce are sad and hurtful for most people going through them. But they are not the end of the world, and can be stepping stones to a fresh start on life.

If a lack of confidence in yourself is a major barrier to your letting go of an unworkable relationship, a good self-help programme for this is *Talk to Yourself*, by Charles Zastrow, published by Prentice-Hall. This paperback devotes a whole chapter to techniques for developing a positive identity. Or again, see a properly trained psychologist.

So far, we have been suggesting what we see as the only good reason for leaving a long-term relationship – you can't make it work well. We have tackled the two common, bad reasons people have for staying in unworkable relationships. Now we would like to knock over the common, bad reasons for quitting relationships.

UNREASONABLE REASONS FOR QUITTING YOUR RELATIONSHIP

1 The eternal triangle

We have never seen a relationship become distressed or break up because one of the partners was having an outside relationship. We have seen people in long-term relationships look outside for what they don't seem to be able to find within their long-term relationships.

An 'affair' is more a symptom of a distressed relationship than a cause of it, although mythical thinking can lead the 'wronged' partner to overreact destructively. Instead, this common event could act as a signal to the couple that it's time to do something constructive to improve their relationship, so that it isn't threatened by the feelings or relationships each partner may have for other people.

Example

John came along to therapy very bewildered that his wife, Anne, had just told him about an affair she had been having.

John believed that their relationship had been good. He couldn't understand why Anne would go off with someone else. He admitted that the passion in their relationship, after eight years, had died; they didn't spend much time together, they were both so busy; and occasionally Anne nagged him about how they never talked any more, but they were still friendly with each other, they didn't fight or anything. Sex had become more and more boring but John believed that Anne wasn't interested.

Anne, on the other hand, had become increasingly dissatisfied with the relationship over time. John spent most of his time at work or playing sport; she never saw him. He usually came home tired, ate dinner and collapsed in front of the TV. When they did go out, they were always with friends and John spent most of the time talking to his mates.

Anne made attempts to tell John how she felt but they were always half-hearted and she stopped when John each time called her a 'nagger'.

Anne would then feel guilty and not mention the subject for a while.

She became involved with another man about six months ago. At first the relationship was exciting and new but now she wants to end it and do something about her relationship with John.

Our rule of thumb is to request a moratorium on outside intimate relationships while the partners are working on improving their relationship. We think this task deserves their relatively undivided attention and commitment.

After that, the extent and nature of your respective involvements in outside relationships should be something you have discussed and reached agreement on. The content of that agreement is up to the individual couple, but its necessity is universal.

2 We have fallen out of love

Feelings do not pop up out of the ground like mushrooms after rain. They are the result of your actions and thoughts. If you stop doing and thinking the things that couples in love do and think, don't be surprised if you stop feeling love towards each other.

Companionate love, the only kind you can base a long-term relationship on, results mostly from regular coupling. The three most common reasons for Australians divorcing are all aspects of neglected coupling. Their sexual relationships are not satisfactory, or they do not spend enough time together, sharing other enjoyable activities.

As you will have gathered by now, these complaints are reversible if both partners are willing to work on them.

Example
Marianne had been married to Charles for ten years. The relationship was pleasant and comfortable for both of them, but Marianne had a nagging doubt that things weren't quite right.

She tried to forget about this feeling but now and then it would pop up. It concerned her that she didn't feel 'in love' with Charles any more.

She had once felt a great passion for him and the relationship. She recognised that these feelings would mellow, but they were now mellowing into indifference.

Charles and Marianne rarely went out as a couple any more. They spent most of their time on individual activities. When they were together they usually had to cope with the children's demands. They never spent an evening or holiday alone together.

Marianne was feeling more and more frustrated and dissatisfied with this situation.

Marianne and Charles were falling into Relationship Myth No. 1, and, as you will recognise, were not spending enough time together as a couple. If they had had more information about how to run a successful long-term relationship, they may never have been in this unhappy situation.

3 This relationship doesn't feel right. Another relationship will be better

Again, feelings result from your thoughts and actions. If this relationship doesn't feel right now, the only way you can know that it can never feel right is to try to change that, by systematically trying the procedures in this programme (or good relationship therapy).

The belief that another relationship must be better is sometimes prompted by the fact that one of the partners is already trying another relationship. A common and dreadful mistake is to compare the on-going relationship, with all of its problems, work and maybe companionate love, with the easy excitement and fun of occasional dates and probably passionate love of an outside relationship.

It's like comparing a car with a roller skate. There is some similarity, but the differences are so big as to make a meaningful comparison impossible. We strongly advise people to keep quite separate the questions of whether or not their present relationship can work, and whether or not some other relationship can work.

Example
Rob had been having an affair with Joanne for twelve months. They saw each other once or twice during the week, usually they went out together and then had sex in Joanne's flat.

Both of them enjoyed the relationship very much, including a good sexual relationship.

Recently, however, Joanne was becoming more and more dissatisfied with this arrangement. She felt that her relationship with Rob was very good and she wanted to make it more permanent.

Rob on the other hand was torn between the enjoyable relationship he had with Joanne and his responsibilities at home to Mary and the kids.

His relationship with Mary had become more and more

dissatisfying. Sex had declined particularly in the last five years. When he and Mary did go out, they never had anything to say to each other. In fact now he avoided going out with Mary and made excuses if she suggested they do. They rarely communicated about important matters, or important feelings. Rob felt that Mary, apart from being a good mother and housekeeper, was boring and uninteresting compared to Joanne.

Rob and Mary were reaching a stage in their relationship where both of them felt it was almost impossible to change their bad feelings. If they had recognised the signs earlier and done something about the problems in their relationship, this may not have occurred.

We strongly discourage people from leaving one long-term relationship in order to go into another one. Leave this relationship if it really can't work. Live by yourself for a while, and get yourself together. Then you give any new relationship a better chance of working in its own right.

The serious flaw in this myth is the belief that changing partners will automatically make your intimate relationship successful. In other words, you are buying into the myth that your present relationship is in trouble because of your present partner.

As we discussed at the beginning of this book, that is rarely true. It is usually the case that **both** partners have contributed to the decline of the relationship through unrealistic expectations and missing or faulty relationship skills.

Example
Ian had had a succession of relationships. Two of his relationships had been more serious than the others and he had married. However all his relationships had ended with the women walking out, saying he was an 'inconsiderate so and so'.

Ian was in despair: he wondered when he was going to find a relationship that would last. He kept thinking over his past relationships, wondering what characteristics a woman that he could get on with would have.

He thought the problem may have lain in the fact that he always felt attracted to good-looking, outgoing, independent women. Maybe he should go for a more 'homey' type of woman. He had tried this with one marriage and she had still walked out.

Ian really needs to evaluate what **he** is doing with his partners in the relationships instead of looking only at the partner as an answer to his problems.

If you simply change relationships, you take the same expectations and skills to the next one, with predictable results. This is clearly shown in the number of second relationships which end in strife and divorce, with both partners saying: 'That's just what happened last time. Why do I keep getting involved with such dreadful people?'

You may as well hone up your relationship skills in **this** relationship. As well as finding out whether this relationship **can** work, you are acquiring skills that will be useful to you in the future, regardless of what happens now.

We have often noticed that the more relationship therapy a couple has done, the better they handle separation and divorce, if that becomes their choice. You need the same skills – communication, fight control, problem solving – to handle the end of a relationship constructively as you do to make it work better.

4 My partner never does what I want him to do

Never? The only thing true about over-generalisations is that they are never true. It may be true that your partner often does not do things that you want her to do, or often does things that you don't want her to do. It's also probably true that you are over-sensitive to these issues if your relationship is distressed.

Couples in distressed relationships will often come along with a string of complaints against each other. That is a sure sign that the relationship is in trouble. All relationships have problems; it is how they are resolved that makes it a good relationship. Couples in distressed relationships do not resolve the problems and then each blames the other for the trouble in the relationship.

Example
'He never asks me out.'
'She never wants to have sex with me.'
'He thinks I am stupid.'
'She always ignores me.'
'He never spends time with the children.'

'She never listens to me.'
'He always goes out without telling me where he is going.'
'She is always nagging me.'

In any case, such complaints are now targets for behaviour-change requests and negotiation. If such attempts don't work, then you might decide you are in the wrong relationship. But the fact that your partner is not your puppet is not a good reason for quitting a relationship.

'BUT WE MUST STAY TOGETHER FOR THE CHILDREN'S SAKE.'

We could have included this with the other bad reasons above for staying in a bad relationship, but it's so common we thought it deserved special attention. Basically, it's rubbish.

Children who lose a parent through death are naturally distressed but rarely harmed by it. Children who 'lose' a parent through divorce are usually both distressed and harmed by the experience. Clearly, it is not the loss of the parent which is potentially harmful, but the manner of the loss.

All too often, the decline of the relationship has been marked by growing hostility between the partners, and that hostility is perpetuated and even increased during and after the divorce. The children get stuck in an emotional no man's land, to be repeatedly fought over by the parents for the sake of minor victories over each other.

Children are not thick. Indeed, they are often remarkably sensitive to the atmosphere at home, despite attempts by the parents to hide or deny their relationship problems. We commonly find that the children have started to show emotional and behavioural signs of stress by the time couples come to us for therapy.

Example
Bill and Cecilia both felt very unhappy about their relationship. The number of fights had increased in frequency and violence over the past year. After each fight they both made an attempt to change things but that never lasted and they wound up exactly where they were before, arguing and fighting.

Cecilia had several times reached the point where she was about to walk out but she stopped each time for the sake of the children.

The children had been very important for both Bill and Cecilia: they wanted the best for them.

Bill and Cecilia had tried to keep their troubles from the children. They played the role of the happy family and tried to keep their fights to times after the children had gone to bed.

However in the last year, Jeremy had begun to wet the bed, at the age of nine; Allan had been doing poorly at school – his teachers said he lacked concentration; and Sara had been very cross and irritable, which was unlike her previous easy going manner.

If you stay together 'for the kids' sake', you teach them several ideas:

No matter how bad a relationship is, you cannot do without one.

It is normal for marriage partners to snipe at and argue with each other.

You should never openly express feelings.

Marriage partners don't feel or share love or affection.

Are these the ideas about relationships that you want to pass on to your children? Remember, your example will speak much more loudly than your words. If this isn't your goal, then don't perpetuate an unworkable relationship 'for the kids' sake'.

If your decision is to separate and divorce, your children will almost certainly be distressed by that, and will show occasional signs of that distress for years to come. It can be hard to be asked, 'Why doesn't Daddy live with us any more?'

But that distress will be less than they will experience trapped in a declining relationship with two adults who just don't want to be with each other. And the process does not have to be harmful. Below we have made some suggestions for approaching separation and divorce constructively. A good self-help resource in this particular area is *You're Divorced but Your Children Aren't*, by T.R. & D. Duncan (Prentice-Hall). You can also get support from organisations like Parents without Partners.

ALTERNATIVES TO DIVORCE

We usually begin relationship therapy by telling distressed couples they have only three real-world choices: do nothing, try to improve the relationship, or call it quits. They cannot avoid making one or other of these choices.

Doing nothing is a real choice, however unwittingly it is made. It has real effects. Typically, doing nothing leads to both partners feeling more hopeless and resentful, and reacting to each other accordingly. The relationship declines further, and the chance of ever improving it gets steadily less.

Sometimes people will effectively be making this choice because they say they cannot make up their minds about what to do. This is more likely when one of the partners has begun another relationship, and working on one relationship appears likely to jeopardise the other.

Our advice remains the same: the longer you perpetuate these limbo situations, the more hurt is done to all the people involved and the more harm is done to all the relationships involved.

Beware of looking for the Phantom Right Answer. In complex human relationships, there is no single Right Answer. Whichever decision you make will be right for some reasons, and wrong for some others. Another decision would be both right and wrong for different sets of reasons.

The best you can aim for is to have thought about your choices carefully, tried things out if appropriate, and made a choice. And then accept that you will feel uncertain and anxious about your choice.

If your decision is to try to improve the relationship, you can try self-help, via this programme, or seek professional help, as discussed above. We add only one piece of advice: while you are working on the relationship, there must be a moratorium on discussion or threats of separation or divorce. Such threats commonly sneak into arguments as another way to clout each other. They are dead ends to genuine discussion and problem solving, and only serve to increase each other's uncertainty about the relationship. While you are working on the relationship, that's what you talk about. If you talk about separation and divorce, that should be because that's what you've decided.

The third choice is to call it quits. Usually this means first separation, and later divorce, although some people put themselves into difficult situations by trying to live separately in the same house while waiting for divorce. For most, the real decision is to separate, and the divorce tends to flow from that.

Beware of the Phantom Trial Separation. Most couples who separate stay separated and get divorced. Usually the suggestion of a 'trial separation' really means, 'I want to separate for good, but I'm not game enough to say so'.

Sometimes a 'trial separation' will be suggested in the sincere belief that the two partners need time to think about the relationship. Well, you can't work at making a relationship better or find out whether that's possible, by practising living apart.

We will begin relationship therapy with a couple who are separated and you can begin self-help if you are separated, but only on the clear understanding that you spend enough time together to try out the relationship skills and exercises as we introduce them. If therapy begins to work, we expect a couple to live together again, because that's the only way they can really decide the possible future of the relationship.

If you really feel you need some breathing space from each other and the relationship, we suggest that should be brief and for clear purposes. Beware of woolly goals like 'thinking about it all'. After the third time through thinking about your relationship, which probably really requires half an hour, you will not get any further with just more thinking. Prolonged attempts at 'thinking' are usually attempts either to postpone an unpleasant decision or to find the Phantom Right Answer.

SHOULD WE CALL IT QUITS?

Here are some brief practical guidelines for considering separation or divorce. If you feel you would like a more detailed discussion of the issues in this chapter, or more extensive self-help advice, we recommend *Divorce*, by John and Nancy Adam. If you are particularly concerned about how to handle events in the best way for any children involved, we recommend *You're Divorced but Your Children*

Aren't, by T.R. & D. Duncan. Both books are published by Prentice-Hall.

1 Take your time making the decision
As we said before, there is only one really good reason for getting out of a relationship: you can't make it work properly. It usually takes time for you to make constructive attempts to make it work or not. A hasty decision to walk out or throw out, made in anger or hurt, is quite likely to be regretted later.

2 Keep using communication skills
It is just as important to level, listen and validate now as ever before. You can still provide each other with support and understanding while you work together on rearranging your relationship.

3 Set aside time to talk
Separation and divorce are nearly always hurtful so there's a strong temptation to avoid talking about them. Avoiding painful issues not only doesn't solve them, it usually makes the situation worse. On the other hand, problems faced up to are often not as bad as you imagine beforehand.

4 Accept that it hurts
It nearly always does. Even when it is obvious that the relationship has been very bad, and has no chance of working, it still usually hurts to call it quits. Be wary of nonsensical self-talk in which you see the end of the relationship as some 'personal failure'. As you will know by now, it takes two people to cause a relationship to decline, even though both of them typically wish it wouldn't.

Help yourself to manage the hurt by rehearsing sensible self-talk, like:

'I expect to feel hurt thinking or talking about the end of our relationship, but I can cope with that. I don't have to deny that feeling, but I also don't have to exaggerate it by dwelling on the bad aspects of the situation, or by increasing any tension between us.'

5 Accept mixed feelings
Nearly everyone has them. Again, no matter how bad the relationship has been, if you finally decide to quit it, you will have some doubts. Re-read our earlier discussion of the Phantom Right Answer, and then stop looking for it.

6 Watch your self-talk

How you feel about your separation or divorce will be largely determined by how you think about it. In this stage of your relationship, as in all the others, beware of the influence of popular myths, this time the Myths of Divorce.

Like, 'Divorce is a Cop-out'. This myth is based on the idea that it is better to suffer nobly forever than to 'give up'. It implies that your relationship is some mountain that you must conquer for your life to have been worthwhile. After all, your only function in this universe is to make this relationship successful, isn't it?

We think there is more to life than martyrdom. For whose sake are you prolonging a hopeless relationship? Really for the sake of your children or partner, or to protect yourself from irrational feelings of failure? Which is the real cop-out?

Or, 'Divorce is a Catastrophe'. Only if you make it one. How you handle your divorce determines how destructive it will be, for all involved. Below are some suggestions on how to handle it constructively. The choice is yours: World War III or a negotiated peace.

7 Make your own decisions

Beware of psychopests, the well-intended but interfering people who want to tell you how to run your life. If you ask five people what to do, you'll get six answers, advanced confusion and a headache.

Welcome emotional support from family or friends, but take advice with a pinch of salt. Even if it really worked for someone else, that doesn't necessarily mean it's appropriate for you. In the end, it's your life, and you have to take final responsibility for how you run it.

8 Tell the kids the truth

Children are not stupid. Even if their parents try to hide conflicts, they will sense that something is wrong. Worrying about the unknown, because it is unexplained, is harder for them to cope with than a simple and honest statement about any present difficulties in the parents' relationship.

If you decide to separate, tell your children. Explain simply and directly that Mum and Dad don't want to live with each other any more, that this decision has nothing to do with the children or their behaviour, and that Mum and Dad both still love the children.

It is sadly necessary for us to advise you strongly not to be tempted to use your children to get at each other. Blackening your partner's character in the eyes of your children may give you some short-term pleasure of revenge, but recognise the price you are asking them to pay for your feelings.

Example

Brian and Sandra had been married for sixteen years. During the past four years Sandra had become increasingly dissatisfied with the relationship she had with Brian. Their children were all teenagers who were starting to live their own lives.

Sandra wanted to work, travel and meet new people. She was particularly interested in a job she had applied for which would involve travelling.

Brian, on the other hand, wanted to stay at home; he wasn't interested in living overseas. He had travelled a lot in the past; now he wished to settle down.

Sandra's and Brian's different expectations in life style caused conflict between them. Each time it occurred they were able to talk about it sensibly but they were never able to find a solution that suited both of them.

Eventually Brian initiated a discussion on the possibility of divorce.

Brian: 'I can understand your desire to work and travel to meet new people but it is something I am not interested in doing. I would like to live with you but I find it too upsetting to have you running off while I would like to sit at home. We both want very different things from our lives now; I wonder if a divorce would be best for both of us.'

Sandra: 'I feel upset at the idea of divorcing but I have also thought about it. We seem to be continually upset with each other, which I have found very tiring. I would, however, like to spend a little time thinking this through. Can we speak tomorrow morning about our decision?'

Brian and Sandra decided to divorce.

After making their decision calmly, despite feeling upset, they had a family conference and informed their children.

You may not have exactly the same reasons for considering divorce as the couple in the above example but you can resolve the issue just as calmly and rationally.

CONSTRUCTIVE DIVORCE

If you follow the guidelines and suggestions above, discuss the situation and alternatives properly, and then decide to end the relationship, the logical aim is to do that as constructively as possible to minimise the hurt for all involved. Here are some suggestions on how to do this. The self-help references above are again relevant.

1 Accept your bad feelings
As above, accept reasonable feelings of hurt, sadness or doubt. But also accept that you will survive them, and they alone are not good reasons to change your mind.

2 Watch your self-talk
Again, how you feel depends on how you think. If you are feeling unreasonably bad, that's almost certainly because you are telling yourself nonsense. Here is a checklist of common but irrational self-talk in divorcing people. If you find yourself thinking like this, we suggest you replace it with the matching, more rational self-talk.

Unhelpful self-talk:
I can't cope by myself.

Helpful self-talk:
Things may be difficult for a while, and I probably will feel bad about that, but I can cope with bad feelings, and I can take constructive steps to make my new life better.

The rotten so-and-so. How could she do this to me? How could she have treated me like that in the past? After all I did for her, and all I put into the relationship.

It does hurt to think of some of the things that went wrong in our relationship, and of its end now, but I can cope with those feelings, and there's no point exaggerating them now by dwelling on the past. I've got to get on with my new life.

I must be a total failure as a person. I've lost this relationship, and I can never make my relationships work. What's wrong with me?	It takes two people to make or break a relationship. Sure, I contributed to what went wrong, but so did he. The best I can do now is try to learn from what went wrong, so I can make my next relationship better.

The other mental exercise that can help you cope with divorce is to ask yourself whether or not you would expect to cope if you suddenly lost your partner through unexpected death. Yes, you would be hurt, and you would grieve, but eventually you would get on with your life. Losing your partner by divorce is not rationally different.

4 Stop rehearsing the past
Running mental movies of past hurts or mistakes has only one effect: it makes you feel bad now. What for? Even if there are lessons for you to learn from reviewing what went wrong in the relationship, you'll probably do that better later when you are over the major hurt of the divorce.

5 Stop blaming
Psychologists are sometimes accused of blaming the parents for everybody's problems. We don't see any value in blaming anybody for anything. Blaming is a value judgement: it says you were 'wrong' or 'evil' to do something. We don't find such value judgements helpful.

We do try to **understand** why something has gone wrong, because that understanding may help you to fix it up or avoid the same mistake in the future. So by all means, try to understand what you or your partner did that contributed to the decline of the relationship. But don't waste your energy in blaming.

6 Get legal advice
Only a lawyer – not your partner and not friends – can really tell you what your legal situation is or what steps to take. Disgruntled spouses are especially inclined to underestimate each other's rights. Divorce is a common enough event for any solicitor to be able either to advise you, or to give you an appropriate referral.

If you don't think you can afford legal fees, approach the nearest community legal advice bureau and ask about legal aid. If you feel up to it, especially if you are both willing to work together on the project, there are quite good do-it-yourself kits advertised in the daily press. You may find these inadequate if you have complicated property or custody questions.

7 Decide on custody

Remember that your children are human beings and not more property to be haggled over. Read again our advice above about being honest with the kids, and not using them to get at each other.

Set aside some time to sit down together and, using your communication and problem-solving skills, work out what arrangements are in the best interests of the children. Here are some questions you will need to consider.

Who really wants responsibility for the children? Caring properly for kids takes time and effort, which can be even more difficult in a single parent family.

Who can provide a better home? Materially? Emotionally? Does one of you travel a lot for your work, meaning you're away a lot? Would it be better to split these tasks, with one of you taking prime responsibility for providing material and financial needs, while the other takes prime responsibility for providing emotional needs.

What do the children want? As far as possible, their wishes should be respected. If this isn't possible, the reasons should be explained to them. Ideally, have a roundtable conference of the family to discuss what's happening and let the children express their preferences.

What visiting rights will apply? Children usually want and benefit from a secure and continuing relationship with the non-custodial parent. This is best achieved by making clear visiting arrangements and sticking to them, or giving the children plenty of notice of any changes. Completely open visiting rights may seem a good idea but they often don't work. Each of you will want to build a new life, probably including new relationships, and unexpected visits to or from your ex-spouse can unfairly interfere with that.

Different families arrive at different solutions for custody and visiting arrangements. Present research suggests one important rule of thumb: children of divorced parents are least likely to show any long-term harmful effects of the divorce if both parents keep active interest in and relationships with the children, however that is arranged.

8 Decide who lives where
This may already have been decided in working out custody of the children. If not, decide now whether one or both of you will move from the home. Preferably make that decision on practical grounds. Does one of you need the home, say, to house the children, or would it be fairest to sell it and share the proceeds?

Occasionally we see couples who try to live separately in the same house, or at least near each other. Frankly, this seems to be an arrangement that will maximise the hurt and uncertainty of the situation. Most people find it easier to cope with divorce if they make a complete and clean break.

AFTER THE DIVORCE

Most divorcees experience some feelings of pain and loneliness after their divorces. In a real sense, it is like the grief you would experience if you lost your partner through death and, like that grief, it is important not to deny those feelings.

Give yourself permission to have these 'normal' feelings. Some divorcees make life difficult for themselves by rushing out, and into bed, with any casual partner they can find, in a sadly desperate attempt to hide from bad feelings, or prove to themselves that there's nothing wrong with their attractiveness.

Example
Jill had moved into a new apartment after separating from her husband.

She still felt very lonely and upset about the separation. To cope with this she had been going out nearly every night to singles bars and clubs. She had met a string of men and subsequently slept with most of them, usually because, after a couple of drinks, she felt lonely, so she asked them to stay.

Jill felt very demoralised by her behaviour. Her self-esteem had been low after the separation and it was getting worse. None of the men she met were very interesting and she felt she was losing her other friends.

Equally, some divorcees make themselves unnecessarily miserable by hiding away from the world, stewing over their dreadful situation and practising irrational self-talk to make themselves depressed.

Example
Harry was now responsible for his children's needs as well as his own, since his divorce. He felt unable to cope with the demands and responsibilities.

By the time he got home at night after work he was tired and worn out. He had to cook dinner, help the kids with their homework and put them to bed. He then read the paper before going to bed.

In the morning the same boring routine began again.

When Harry did find himself with some spare time, he felt miserable and listless. He sat around wishing he and his wife could get back together again. Things weren't good then but they seemed better than living alone.

Harry became more and more depressed. He discouraged friends dropping around and never went out any more, using the need to look after the kids as an excuse.

There is a reasonable path between these extremes: accept a reasonable level of bad feelings, and gradually rebuild a new life to replace lost rewarding and enjoyable activities and relationships. Don't be in a hurry to find another intimate relationship. You give any future relationship its best chance of working if you get yourself together first.

Sarah had been separated for six months. She was living by herself with her two children. She had never worked before but in the last month had finally found a job working in a shop. She felt very pleased with herself.

Since she had been working, she had had a girl come in three afternoons a week to tidy up, pick the children up from school and cook dinner. On the other two nights the children went to a friend's place after school.

Sarah was spending most of her wage on living expenses but she felt it was worthwhile; it enabled her to get out of the house and meet people and she felt better about herself while she was working. She also joined a painting class on Saturday mornings, and was studying English one night a week.

At times Sarah felt upset about being separated but she coped with this; she was happy to be meeting new people and getting involved in things she had always wanted to do.

One question you will need to resolve for yourself after the divorce is the nature and extent of your relationship with your previous spouse. Sometimes divorcees feel they ought to be able to be good friends, and that it would be immature or ungracious of them to want less.

In fact, most divorcing couples eventually develop polite but fairly distant relationships with each other. This seems a reasonable goal, considering that their relationships have often come to an end because of considerable bad feelings between them. If you can both feel comfortably friendlier than that, good luck to you, but neither of you should feel obliged to do so.

Some minimum of co-operation in the relationship is desirable if you have children since you may need to arrange and revise custody or visiting arrangements from time to time. If one of you has custody, the non-custodial parent should accept that the custodial parent has prime say in the children's lives.

Ideally, you should discuss any major decisions affecting the children, and let them know you have the discussions, so they know you are both still actively interested in their welfare. But if you cannot agree on an issue, the custodial parent should have the last say.

There is no need for you to try to match your two new households in terms of what is or is not expected of the children. Kids routinely learn that different codes or styles of behaviour apply in different places. But don't make an issue of such differences, using them as a means of running down your ex-spouse in the children's eyes. You are just different on that point, and you and your children should be able to accept such differences.

Finally, you will need to face up constructively to the task of rebuilding those parts of your life changed or lost by your divorce. Apart from losing the relationship itself, divorcees sometimes also lose activities or friendships that were previously shared with their spouses, or are lost by moving.

A marked loss of rewarding activities and relationships can lead to depression if you do nothing about it. So it is important that you take constructive if gradual steps to replace lost activities and relationships. This can be difficult if you are the custodial parent of young children but you will not be doing them any favours if you make yourself depressed.

At first some divorcees find their new state quite strange, particularly if they have been married for a long time. They have been accustomed to their role as married persons, and now aren't sure what they are or how they are expected to behave.

This situation is made more difficult by the lack of social facilities for or approval of older, single people in our society. Older divorcees may feel anxious about trying to establish new relationships because they fear looking foolish.

Against these sorts of fears, you can tell yourself, quite honestly, that your divorce gives you a chance to explore new activities, and new roles for yourself. Take your time and experiment with some of these. Work out a new lifestyle that suits you.

Two good self-help manuals for this are *Coping: A Survival Manual for Women Alone*, by Martha Yates (Prentice-Hall), and *First Person Singular: Living the Good Life Alone*, by Dr Stephen Johnson (Signet Books). There are also organisations for divorcees and single parents which can provide practical and emotional support. Don't let unreasonable embarrassment stop you from using them.

By now you will be expecting us to say that how you feel about your new life will be largely determined by how you think about it, so we won't disappoint you. Watch your self-talk. If you find you are feeling unreasonably bad for much of the time, make a consistent attempt to think more rationally about your situation. If you can't do that for yourself, do get some help.

A note on the theory and research behind our approach in this manual

We have tried to provide enough detailed advice and examples in this book for a couple to use it as a self-help manual, and it should successfully fill this function for many people who wish to improve or enhance their relationship.

The research on the effectiveness of self-help manuals is mixed (Glasgow & Rosen, 1979) and there is a general conclusion that the most effective and safe use of such manuals may be as an adjunct to therapy. A well-designed self-help manual can greatly enhance and facilitate therapy by providing easily assimilable and reviewable information, numerous relevant examples, and explicit assignments. This reduces reliance on the clients' memory of discussions in therapy, makes clear the agreed assignments which we believe are essential to generalise therapeutic gains into the clients' life situation, and thus contributes to cost-effective therapy.

To this end, we have included the following brief review of the theoretical and research bases of our approach to relationship therapy. This review is intended to help relationship counsellors and therapists make optimum use of the manual in their face-to-face counselling or therapy.

Traditional theories of marriage

Early marriage counselling relied heavily on the notions of personality disorder as a means of explaining disharmony in marriage. Research over the last twenty years cast serious doubt on the idea that people have stable, measurable 'personalities' at all. It now seems clear that people's behaviour often reflects situational factors as much as stable tendencies to respond in certain ways. The relevant implication of this is the need to examine the situational influences resulting from being in a relationship.

The marital therapy based on the traditional approach, which focussed on 'curing' the 'sick' partner, was marked by a singular lack of both supporting evidence and success.

Developments in behaviour therapy shifted the focus from analysis of internal characteristics to detailed examination of external influences on human behaviour. In marital research, the behavioural consequences of an individual's actions were seen as important in determining the success of a relationship. A social interaction approach to marriage developed and no longer was individual personality held to be crucial in the outcome of marriage.

Social learning approach to marriage

The social learning theorists at places like Oregon University introduced a refreshingly practical and effective note by focussing on the behaviours emitted by the two partners within the relationship and their reciprocal influence – what they did, or did not do, with and to each other – and established the need for skills like communication, coupling, problem solving and fight control.

The social learning approach encourages the couple to focus on each other's behaviour, rather than on their 'personalities'. Constructive feedback, aimed at the other's behaviour, gives them the chance of changing it if they want to. Destructive feedback, aimed at the other person, goes nowhere. It only invites similar retaliation and a further deterioration of the relationship.

Relational therapy based on this approach therefore focusses on what is called the dyad – the two people and the interaction between them. It has concentrated on teaching them more skilful ways of interacting, and has been marked by considerably more success than traditional marital counselling. Apart from the obvious cases where one of the partners had a severe psychological problem, such as alcoholism, this seemed to put an end to the 'personality' approach to marital counselling.

Jacobson & Margolin (1979), in a review of the behavioural marital approach, concluded that the Oregon type of programme (Weiss *et al.*, 1980) despite some methodological problems, had demonstrated that it was the most effective strategy for treating distressed relationships.

Cognitive behavioural approach to marriage

While Bob was working with the Oregon group a few years ago, he was struck by the fact that some couples could practise the appropriate relationship skills, under the supervision of the therapist in the clinic, but didn't seem to be able to apply them at home. They made no real progress in therapy, and would usually eventually split up.

Around the same time, clinical psychology was undergoing a marked change by becoming willing, and then enthusiastic, to look at the role of cognitive variables in dysfunctional behaviour and therefore in therapy. This trend has burgeoned into the field of cognitive-behavioural therapy which we see as a desirable combination of an experimental approach to troubled behaviour with a humanistic appreciation of what goes on in human behaviour rather than non-human.

It was the limited effectiveness of a strictly behavioural approach with these couples that led us to look for a possible role in relationship dysfunction for thoughts, attitudes and beliefs, and so eventually our research project (Evans, 1980).

Jacobson & Margolin (1979) argued that in a behavioural approach to marriage it was unnecessary directly to assess individuals' perceptions and expectations. It was believed that individuals' perceptions would automatically realign as a consequence of their behaviour-change. This may be an unwarranted assumption, given the evidence for a general capacity to express, if not hold, beliefs and attitudes contradictory to one's overt behaviour (Triandis, 1971).

Even if this assumption were true, it does not mean that direct cognitive change may not also enhance a behavioural approach. The existing behavioural marital programmes did not assess cognitions or include direct cognitive change as one of their procedures (Weiss, 1980; Gottman *et al.*, 1976), though they may have assumed it occurred through overt behaviour-change and frequently refer to cognitive aspects of relationships.

Our research assessed the difference between the **internal** dialogue (attitudes, beliefs and self-statements) of distressed and non-distressed couples. Secondly, distressed couples were seen in therapy which included direct cognitive change procedures, and the internal dialogue of each individual was assessed again post-therapy.

In summary, the results from our research indicated that it could be desirable to include procedures for cognitive change in behavioural marital therapy because of (a) the clear difference in self-statements between distressed and non-distressed couples; and (b) the change in self-statements which accompanied successful progress in therapy.

Our view is that relational success depends on two sets of factors: the relational skills employed by the couple, and the self-talk used by each of the individual partners. The relationship myths discussed in this book are one example of that self-talk; another important one turned out to be self-esteem.

The content of this manual reflects this view of the determinants of relationship success and thus, we believe, enjoys good research support. This does not mean that we think the programme is infallible or a panacea for relationship ills, nor that it represents the last word in relationship therapy. We do believe that a relationship counsellor or therapist can implement the programme spelled out in this manual, comfortable in the knowledge that it has a reasonable research base and represents the current state of the art of relationship therapy.

Suggestions on how to use this book

We believe that it is important for any clinician to have a good understanding of the theoretical basis of the procedures they are using. The review above only summarises the social learning and cognitive behaviour modification bases to cognitive-behavioural marital therapy. References are given at the end of this section if you feel you need to read further in these areas.

Once you have some understanding of the theoretical approaches, it may be important that you rehearse teaching the practical skills set out in this manual before attempting to use them with clients. Therapy is an essentially practical exercise. Attempting novel or complicated procedures in therapy can be threatening to the therapist, and this may in turn severely limit the effectiveness of the therapy. If you feel the need, the best strategy would be to avail yourself of a practical training programme in this area. If that is not possible, we strongly recommend practising the procedures with colleagues, through role-playing, before using them with distressed couples.

Marital counselling or therapy can proceed by using one chapter as the basis for one or more consultations. The couple can be asked to read the chapter before the consultation, which focusses on modelling and practice of the skills in that chapter, and the exercises in the chapter can then be set as assignments. The next session can be spent reviewing practice by the couple and discussing any problems that they are having.

We find this a very successful approach to therapy. The client is able to digest the new material at home; s/he is able to refer back again and again to the correct information; there is no need to rely on memory; and the client, if need be, can recycle the programme again and again without the necessity of continuing to see a therapist.

Most couples should be able to use the programme with varying amounts of guidance from a therapist. Of course, individual couples will vary on how many consultations they need. We often find couples who are not very distressed, and proficient readers, may only need to see a therapist three or four times. This is sufficient for them to continue self-help, using the manual, after therapy.

On the other hand, couples who are very distressed may require a number of sessions to break the initial dead-lock or stand-off in their relationship, but then they can begin to use the self-help programme successfully. Couples who are unable or unwilling to read much will obviously need more direct guidance.

Evaluation of self-help

It has become increasingly evident in the literature that self-help programmes need to be evaluated. With this in mind the manuscript of this book was used in a research project by a Master of Psychology student at La Trobe University. Preliminary findings only are available at time of this publication, but they indicate that couples who considered themselves distressed were able to use the book effectively without any assistance from a therapist. But, as we have warned in the body of the book, couples who are very distressed, or have poor fight control skills, usually find it difficult to benefit from a self-help programme alone.

References

Evans, L. Cognitive Factors In Functional Dysfunctional Relationships and Therapy, La Trobe University, Melbourne, 1980 (unpublished thesis).

Glasgow, R. & Rosen, G. 'Self-help Behaviour Therapy Manuals: Recent developments and Clinical Usage.' *Clinical Behaviour Therapy Review*, Vol. 1, No. 1, Spring 1979.

Gottman, J., *et al*. *A Couple's Guide To Communication*, Research Press, 1976.

Jacobson, N. & Margolin, G. *Marital Therapy*, Brunner/Mazel, 1979.

Liberman, R., *et al*. Handbook Of Marital Therapy, Plenum Press, 1980.

Montgomery, R.B., *et al*. Enabling Sexual Health Through Self-Centered Behaviour Change. *Current Problems in Obstetrics and Gynecology* (Monograph), 1978, 6, No. 1.

Triandis, H. *Attitude and Attitude Change*, John Wiley and Sons, Inc., 1971.

Weiss, B. *Coupling*, BMA Audiocassettes, 1980.

234

Acknowledgements

Our thanks to the following for permission to reproduce illustrations:

To Boomer Books, Australia, for the cartoon from *Sunday Snake, created and drawn by SOLS* (Allan Salisbury); to Allan Foley Pty Ltd for the three cartoons from *The Wizard of Id* by Brant Parker and Johnny Hart; to Murray Publishers Pty Ltd for the illustration from *Romantic Confessions*; to Robson Books Ltd for the three cartoons from *Inside Woody Allen, Selections from the Comic Strip*, drawn by Stuart Hemple; and to United Feature Syndicate for the *Peanuts* cartoon.